ARABIC   ASTRONOMY   BANKING   BEE-KEEPING   BIOLOGY
ANISATION   CALCULUS   CANASTA   CARPENTRY   CHEMISTRY
COMMERCIAL CORRESPONDEN   TO
KING   CRICKET   DRAWING   UTTON
ELECTRICITY IN THE HO   IDERY
ENGLISH RENASCENCE TO   ANTIC
EVERYDAY FRENCH   TO E   D FLY
SE BOOK   GARDENING   HY OF
ONARY   GERMAN GRAMM   GOLF
GOOD FARM ACCOUNTING   GOOD FARM CROPS   GOOD FARMING
T FARMING   GOOD GRASSLAND   GOOD AND HEALTHY ANIMALS
GOOD POULTRY KEEPING   GOOD SHEEP FARMING   GOOD SOIL
E HINDUSTANI   HISTORY: ABRAHAM LINCOLN ALEXANDER THE
AU CONSTANTINE COOK CRANMER ERASMUS GLADSTONE AND
MILTON PERICLES PETER THE GREAT PUSHKIN RALEIGH RICHELIEU
DROW   EMENT
LIAN   ETTER
ENGIN   ANICS
DERN   ORING
HILOSO   HYSICS
LUMBI   UBLIC
RECKO   SSIAN

ITS N   AND PURPOSE   SOCCER   SPANISH   SPE   AND
SWA   SWEDISH   TEACHING   THINKING   TRIG   METRY
BRI   H RAILWAYS FOR BOYS   CAMPING FOR BOYS AND GIRLS
FOR GIRLS   MODELMAKING FOR BOYS   NEEDLEWORK FOR GIRLS
OYS AND GIRLS   SAILING AND SMALL BOATS FOR BOYS AND GIRLS
ORK FOR BOYS   ADVERTISING & PUBLICITY   ALGEBRA   AMATEUR
ING   BIOLOGY   BOOK-KEEPING   BRICKWORK   BRINGING UP
NTRY   CHEMISTRY   CHESS   CHINESE   COMMERCIAL ARITHMETIC
RAVELLING   TO COMPOSE MUSIC   CONSTRUCTIONAL DETAILS
JG   DUTCH   DUTTON SPEEDWORDS   ECONOMIC GEOGRAPHY
ST   EMBROIDERY   ENGLISH GRAMMAR   LITERARY APPRECIATION
VAL   ROMANTIC REVIVAL   VICTORIAN AGE   CONTEMPORARY
FISHING   TO FLY   FREELANCE WRITING   FRENCH   FRENCH
OUSE   GEOGRAPHY OF LIVING THINGS   GEOLOGY   GEOMETRY
ASE BOOK   GOLF   GOOD CONTROL OF INSECT PESTS   GOOD
FARM CROPS   GOOD FARMING   GOOD FARMING BY MACHINE
D   GOOD AND HEALTHY ANIMALS   GOOD MARKET GARDENING
GOOD SHEEP FARMING   GOOD SOIL   GOOD ENGLISH   GREEK
ORY: ABRAHAM LINCOLN   ALEXANDER THE GREAT BOLIVAR BOTHA
RANMER ERASMUS GLADSTONE AND LIBERALISM HENRY V JOAN OF
AT PUSHKIN RALEIGH RICHELIEU ROBESPIERRE THOMAS JEFFERSON
HOME NURSING   HORSE MANAGEMENT   HOUSEHOLD DOCTOR
URNALISM   LATIN   LAWN TENNIS   LETTER WRITER   MALAY
ONENTS   WORKSHOP PRACTICE   MECHANICS   MECHANICAL
MORE GERMAN MOTHERCRAFT   MOTORING   MOTOR CYCLING
APHY   PHYSICAL GEOGRAPHY   PHYSICS   PHYSIOLOGY   PITMAN'S
JESE   PSYCHOLOGY   PUBLIC ADMINISTRATION   PUBLIC SPEAKING

· · · AND HE WILL BE
YET WISER *Proverbs 9.9*

ENGLISH LITERATURE

VOLUME III
1650–1780

The Teach Yourself
History of
English Literature

is complete in
six volumes

The Teach Yourself
History of
English Literature

THE ENGLISH RENASCENCE TO
THE ROMANTIC REVIVAL
1650–1780

based on the original work of
Arthur Compton-Rickett, M.A., LL.D.
and edited throughout by
PETER WESTLAND

VOLUME III

THE ENGLISH UNIVERSITIES PRESS LTD.
LONDON

First printed 1950

*Printed in Great Britain for the English Universities Press, Limited,
by Richard Clay and Company, Ltd., Bungay, Suffolk*

FOREWORD

THE six volumes of *The Teach Yourself History of English Literature* are planned so that they may form one complete work, with each volume complete in itself and yet connecting up with the lines of thought which begin in the first volume and are illustrated all the way through to the end of the series. Thus it is possible for a reader to concentrate on a single volume, for his own purposes, or to read the books in almost any order. The reader who wishes, however, to study the full course should begin with the first volume, since this lays down essential principles of literary appreciation and has been written as the key volume to this account of English literature.

The author of the first and last volumes has prepared the other volumes by condensing the excellent *A History of English Literature* by Dr. Arthur Compton-Rickett, to which summary he has added, both within the text and additionally to it, his own material and comment. In doing this he has tried to preserve as much of the author's style of narrative as possible, with its skilful sketching in of background, lively interest in biographical detail, and that remarkable faculty by which Dr. Compton-Rickett unfailingly interested his readers in the books and authors he discussed. In this last gift he was outstanding among really valuable critics of this century.

The final volume strikes a balance between critical selection of contemporary literature and the recording of works which the reading public and its critics have found notable. By writing it in this way it has been possible to give as much valuation of contemporary work as may be sensibly made, while at the same time indicating to readers books and movements and aspirations which, at this point, each of us must appraise for himself. A general picture of contemporary fiction, non-fiction, poetry, and drama is given in the text; the use of the index brings together the details given about particular authors.

For permission to use Dr. Compton-Rickett's work the kindness of his publishers, Messrs. Thos. Nelson & Sons, is gratefully acknowledged.

CONTENTS

Chapter One

Introduction to an Age

You that delight in wit and mirth
  And love to hear such news
As comes from all parts of the earth,
  Dutch, Danes, and Turks and Jews,
I'll send ye to a rendezvous
  Where it is smoking new;
Go, hear it at a Coffee House,
  It cannot but be true.

THOMAS JORDAN (1675)

ABOUT the middle of the seventeenth century a change
began to come over the spirit of English literature.
This change was due to no mere fluctuation of literary
fashion but was deeply rooted in the life of the time.
The age of the Renascence was an age of spiritual and
material expansion. Englishmen realised for the
first time their solidarity as a nation; and, released
suddenly from Continental struggles, especially from
the dread of Spanish supremacy, they found an out-
let for their excited emotions in drama and song.
Loyalty to Elizabeth became an article of faith;
pride and delight in their country's past a religious
creed.

But the emotional fervour was too high-pitched to
last. Already in the early years of the seventeenth

century its splendid exuberance had degenerated into extravagance and violence. The great minds in the closing years of the age, like Bacon and Milton, reflect in their writings the dawn of fresh interests. The purification of civic and political life emerges more and more into the forefront. Shakespeare and Ben Jonson stand aloof from the political problems of the hour. Bacon and Milton are active politicians no less than great writers; but until the Restoration the full significance of this change is not realised. It meets us first of all in the later poems of Abraham Cowley, and in the polished verse of Edmund Waller and Sir John Denham; it frankly and unmistakably proclaims itself a new note in our literature with the coming of Dryden.

Increasingly during the seventeenth century were men's thoughts directed to problems of civic and national life. The wild, speculative interests and imaginative fervour of the Renascence gave place to a practical application of these ideals to actual existence; and naturally enough literature itself became involved with the problems of practical politics. France no less than England shared in this reaction from Romanticism and, at this juncture, political conditions connected with the Restoration brought the influence of France into special contact with English life and letters.

One may speak, therefore, of three features in the literature of the new age. The triumph of the classical idea was, after all, a natural result of the Renascence.

The Romantic spirit had been aroused, among other things, by a study of Greek and Roman classics, and, while it was the "substance" that excited men at first, when the early exhilaration had worn off the "methods" of the old writers attracted more and more attention. It was seen even in Elizabeth's day that the weakness of Romanticism lay in its lack of form, its variability, its proneness to extravagance and turgidity.

None saw this more clearly than Jonson and his influence was, as we have noted, thrown entirely on the classical side.

This classicism was fostered and encouraged by the political needs of the age; but even then the change might have been more gradual, less decisive, had it not been for the fact that a brilliant set of writers had arisen in France, actuated by classical methods, who exerted a profound influence on the literature of Europe. The influence on England was especially marked, for Court reasons. Much of Charles's exile had been spent in France; he had been attracted towards its literature and did his best to enforce the ideals he saw there, thus influencing English literature. Psychologically the new spirit involved the substitution of the critical for the imaginative spirit.

The new spirit, however, is above all critical and analytic, not creative and sympathetic; it brings the intellect rather than the poetic imagination into play. And the merits of the new school are to be found in its intellectual force and actuality; just as its demerits lie in its lack of deep imagination, and tendency to deal with manners and superficialities rather than with elemental things and the larger issues of life.

Obviously, then, this change was better adapted to a kind of literature which aimed especially at clearness, conciseness, and concentrated force. The less attractive aspect of this ideal is seen in the verse of the day, the finer and more valuable aspects in its prose.

The object of the leading writers of the time was to avoid extravagance and emotionalism. This in many cases they did so successfully as to suppress altogether the emotional and basic qualities of great poetry, though their method found congenial expression in satire.

Poetry, starved of emotional sustenance, had to fall back on epigram, but the " good-sense " ideal formulated in 1673 by Boileau was an admirable one for prose that had suffered from Romantic extravagances. For if we examine the aims of the prose-writers of the day, we shall find that their supreme object is to be simple in style and natural in manner.

In the drama alone, which has come to be a courtier's game, is artificiality of prose upheld. There, for the sake of amusement, lucidity and directness are made subsidiary to brilliance of wit and stylic graces.

Summing up, therefore, the aspects of the change, we may say : There was (1) the academic aspect— the substitution of Classicism for Romanticism; (2)

the political aspect, due (*a*) to the general influence of France at this time, and (*b*) to the particular influence through the medium of the King and his Court; (3) the psychological aspect that underlay these, signifying surely more than a change of fashion—a change of attitude. Influencing all of them was the general drift of the age towards matters of civil and national interest.

Before noting how far this literary revolution is expressed in the literature of the time, it may be well to review the external changes that took place in the new age.

For long-continuing and virulent assault, the Plague which broke out in Tudor times and persisted through the greater part of the seventeenth century exceeded the Sweating Sickness of 1506, and in some respects even the Black Death of 1349. The people fell as thick as leaves in autumn when they are shaken by a mighty wind, wrote a contemporary. The main calamity of the Plague fell upon London.

Scarcely had the horror burst on the City, in 1665, and withdrawn to fester in the slums, than the Great Fire began by an outbreak at the house of the King's baker in Pudding Lane. Pepys recorded how, at three o'clock on the morning of September 2, maids who had been sitting up " to get things ready against our feast to-day " roused him to tell of a fire they saw in the City. Pepys slipped on his nightgown, watched the fire for a time, and went back to bed.

Full daylight and reports coming in gave him a suspicion that the fire was of greater extent than he had supposed. He went out to see for himself, and was shocked to find people flinging their belongings on to lighters on the Thames and fleeing from the blaze, which was by now leaping from street to street of the timber, lath, and plaster houses.   Even now, however, it did not occur to him that the fire was unlikely to burn itself out or to be stayed by the means adopted to check it.

If Pepys was slow to realise the disastrous nature of the fire, many other Londoners were even slower. No organised effort was made to stay the burning, everyone being fully occupied in removing their goods first to a neighbouring house and then farther on and farther on still, until in most cases the all-embracing flames had their way at last.   It was not until after Pepys had taken boat for White Hall and reported to the King and the Duke of York, that the diarist's obviously sensible suggestion—to pull down the houses before the fire—was adopted.   However, probably nothing would have been of real avail. The houses were too " full of matter for burning, as pitch and tar, in Thames Street; and warehouses of oyle, and wines and brandy and other things ".

By now it was twelve o'clock and dinner-time. Directly the meal was over Pepys and his friend Moone walked into the City, to find the streets packed with horses and carts laden with goods " ready to run over one another and removing goods from one burnt house to another. They are now removing out of Canning Street (which received goods in the morning) into Lombard Street and further."

From that time the disaster increased in immensity. When Pepys, his wife, and a few friends met in St. James's Park in the afternoon and went onto the river, it was easy enough to see why so little could be done to stop the progress of the fire. " All over the Thames, with one's faces in the wind, you were almost burned with a shower of fire drops." By night-time the thing had become " a most horrid, malicious, bloody flame ".

> " We staid till, it being darkish, we saw the fire as only one entire arch of fire from this to the other side of the bridge, and in a bow up the hill for an arch of above a mile long. It made me weep to see it. The churches, houses and all on fire, and flaming at once; and a horrid noise the flames made, and the cracking of the houses at their ruine. So home with a sad heart.
> " September 3.—About four o'clock in the morning my Lady Batten sent me a cart to carry away all my money and plate and best things to Sir W. Rider's at Bednallgreene."

During the whole of September 4 the fire blazed on. " Now begins the practice of blowing up houses in Tower Street, those next the Tower, which at first did frighten people more than anything." On the 5th the destruction had reached Barking Church, " which is the bottom of our lane ". So Pepys collected his £2350 worth of gold pieces and carried his good dame away to Woolwich. As it turned out, the precaution was unnecessary, for at the porch of Barking Church the flames were stayed.

So much for East London.

Unfortunately, the City and the district reaching towards Westminster were faring worse. The Exchange was in ruins, Cheapside and Newgate Market all burned. Throughout the day and night of September 6 the same tale of utter desolation was being told everywhere. On the 7th the progress had been stayed, and Pepys ventured to explore as far as the Strand.

> " A miserable sight of Paul's Church, with all the roofs fallen, and the body of the quire fallen into St. Fayth's, Paul's School also, Ludgate and Fleet-street. My father's house, and the church and a good part of the Temple, all in ruins."

The Great Fire of London had entailed a loss of upwards of ten millions sterling. Four City gates, eighty-nine churches, 400 streets, 13,200 houses were destroyed. There was nothing for it but to rebuild the town upon the hot ashes.

The opportunity made the man—Christopher Wren.

The task which Wren set himself was to endow the Gothic pile with the vesture of its old-time sanctity. Before any headway could be made towards the carrying out of the recommendations contained in the elaborate report, however, the Great Plague overtook London. Wren chose to leave England and live in Paris until the earlier conditions in his own country were restored. He was still known as " the Astronomy Professor", but during the visits to the French capital the essential features of Wren's architectural style were developed.

A letter from Christopher Wren to his friend Dr. Bateman proves clearly what a great part the Palace of the Louvre must have played in this respect.

> "I have busied myself [he writes] in surveying the most esteemed Fabricks of Paris and the Country round; the Louvre for a while was my daily object, where no less than a thousand Hands are constantly employed in the Works, some in laying mighty Foundations, some in raising the Stories, Columns, Entablements, etc., with vast Stones by great and useful Engines; others in Carving, Inlaying of Marbles, Plaistering, Painting, Gilding, etc., which altogether make a School of Architecture the best, probably, of this day in Europe."

It was with the memory of Perrault's great building ever before him that Wren came to the task of rebuilding the Cathedral Church of St. Paul after the Great Fire.

It is, however, typical of the philosophic breadth of vision of Wren that he was by no means content to merely suggest the building of a new St. Paul's. Both Evelyn and Wren set to work upon plans for the rebuilding of a new London directly the extent of the damage was realised. Evelyn mentions that Wren was the quicker in placing a scheme before Charles II.

Unfortunately, Wren's scheme for the rebuilding of London upon a definite plan fared less well than his refashioned cathedral. Lack of sufficient funds, the innate conservatism of the citizens of London, and the anxiety to " get something done ", proved obstacles which even Wren's level-headed enthusiasm could not overcome. Nevertheless, by means of his wonderful series of City churches, the architect of St. Paul's left almost as definite an impression upon London as if he had, in truth, designed the whole.

Imagine London without the steeples of St. Bride's, Fleet Street; of St. Mary-le-Bow, Cheapside; and the spire of St. Margaret Pattens—to mention only three of the fifty churches which Wren rebuilt after the Fire. Seventeen have since been taken down and others destroyed by war, but the rest form as enduring a monument to the memory of Christopher Wren as does St. Paul's itself.

Wren died on February 25, 1723. It had been his custom to drive to the Cathedral once a year and sit for a while within the great pile. After one of these visits he returned to his home at Hampton Court. A short while later he was found by his servant dead in his chair. He had passed away in his sleep. The body was laid in the crypt of St. Paul's.

Si monumentum requiris, circumspice.

The characteristics of an age are more faithfully reflected in its imaginative literature than in its formal histories and chronicles. Pope reflects the hard brilliance, the somewhat facile optimism of his generation in much the same way as Tennyson mirrors in his work the religious perplexities and ideals of

Victorian England; and Addison is the Thackeray of his age, in his pictures of the tastes, the fashions, and the follies of the " Town ".

We are approaching now the existence in London of a definite literary class. The poet, the dramatist of the age preceding, depended for his livelihood on a patron.

Patronage still existed, and Pope made his fortunes by what has been called " a kind of joint-stock patronage ", where the aristocratic patron found it convenient to induce his friends to subscribe towards the maintenance of the poet. But the older system was dying out.

At first the poet or the pamphleteer attached himself to some influential Minister, using his pen on behalf of this gentleman's cause. Afterwards, when the Minister found he could get his work done more cheaply than by hiring men of taste, the literary man was thrown upon the suffrages of a public then rising into existence.

The coffee-houses, and later the clubs, were centres around which radiated the thoughtful and intelligent. What Addison did to systematise the fluctuating sentiments and opinions of these will be seen hereafter. It is sufficient to note here that politicians, lawyers, clergymen, literary men, met at these places and discussed the problems of the hour. Thus the author and his public were forced into intimate proximity. If you admired a man's writing, you hastened to his coffee-house, where you might hear him holding forth to his own special friends.   Perhaps you brought with you a companion.   Thus the circle of discipleship grew.

What of the coffee-house, which plays so important a share in the life of the day?

It arose in this fashion.

The coffee-house was the lineal descendant of the barbers' shops, the University dining and debating halls, and the taverns of the Middle Ages.   Here had been the home of the idea; the "baiting-place of wit"; the forge where the rough thought was welded into policy.   Here the political philosopher could hob-nob with the demagogue.

Coffee was introduced into London in 1657 by a Turkish merchant who set up his coffee-house in Lombard Street, with a portrait of himself as a sign over the door.   "That excellent, and by all physicians approved, China drink . . . Tea" was to be had, as well as "Cophee", but the former was a very expensive luxury as yet and was regarded, much as tobacco was on its introduction, as a medicine.   Tea, or Tee, was pronounced as "Tay".   Pope refers to:

> . . . Gentle Anna, whom three realms obey,
> Does sometimes council take, and sometimes Tea.

Coffee-houses now multiplied rapidly and soon each house had its distinctive clientele—lawyers favouring one, politicians another, and so forth. The famous "Wills'" in Covent Garden (the west corner of Bow Street) was patronised by Pepys and

Dryden. This place was termed the "Wits Coffee-house". Dryden was an agreeable, good-natured, somewhat self-opinionated man. He enjoyed a great reputation as a conversationalist, in much the same way as did Addison, who succeeded him.

The host of the coffee-house hears all the town gossip and to him naturally the visitor turns upon his entrance : "What news have you, master ? "

Here is a contemporary picture of the West End life (1722) :

> "We rise at nine, and those that frequent great men's levees found entertainment at them till eleven; or, as in Holland, go to tea tables. About twelve the 'beau monde' assembles in several coffee- or chocolate-houses, the best of which are the 'Cocoa Tree' and 'White's' Chocolate-House, 'St. James', 'The Smyrna', . . . Coffee-houses, and all these so near to one another that in less than an hour you see the company of them all. We are carried to these places in chairs, which are here very cheap, a guinea a week, or one shilling an hour, and your chairman serves you as porter to run errands. . . . If it is fine weather we take a turn in the park till two, when we go to dinner. . . . The general way here is to make a party at the Coffee-house to go to dine at the Tavern, where we sit till six, when we go to the plays unless you are invited to the table of some great man."

Politicians met here, but they had little circles or clubs of their own, and these met often in taverns. The Tory "October Club" met in a tavern at Westminster, the Whig "Kit-cat Club" in a Strand tavern.[1]

---

[1] The "Cat and Fiddle", the shop of a pastry-cook named Christopher Kat.

Theologians and scientists did not disdain the coffee-house. Sir Isaac Newton repaired of an evening to the " Grecian "; and Laurence Sterne preached lay sermons there—probably more interesting than his formal discourses. On one occasion, it is said, he gave out as his text : " It is better to go into the house of mourning than into the house of feasting," and continued : " I dispute that ! " Which we may well believe.

The satirists of the day did not spare coffee. One of them " calls on Ben Jonson's manly ghost, and the noble phantoms of Beaumont and Fletcher, who drank pure nectar ", with " rich canary ennobled ", while these coffee men, these " sons of nought ", gave up the pure blood of the grape for a filthy drink—" syrup of soot, essence of old shoes ".

The influence of the coffee-houses as centres for politics is well illustrated by the attempt of Charles to suppress them in 1675. But the regulation was not enforced, so strong was the feeling against it.

The coffee-house at the time was, as we see, the school of wit and dialectic. What the tavern had been to the sixteenth century, the coffee-house was to the seventeenth and eighteenth. It reached the height of its popularity in the eighteenth, but before its close had passed into practical oblivion.

At one time, it is said, there were no fewer than 3000 coffee-houses in London and these resorts were for all sorts and conditions of men. Each profession, almost each business, had its particular rendezvous. In the better class smoking was allowed; and conversation was compulsory. You paid your twopence for a cup of coffee or tea and then chatted to a neighbour.

The well-known writers of the day congregated at these places and talked to their friends—not infrequently at them. It was at a coffee-house that Pope found Dryden; and here it was that Addison discoursed to a select circle and Johnson delivered many of his sententious periods.

So opinions were formed and circulated.

But potent as were the semi-public meetings in the tavern and the coffee-house for the distribution of news and opinions, they were insufficient for the general needs. A debating agency of an even more public sort was required. During the seventeenth century London folk came slowly to understand that none was more promising than the newspaper, " an open Forum where all mortals vent their opinions, state their grievance; a Forum free to every citizen who has three fingers and a smattering of grammar ", as Carlyle put it in an oft-quoted passage.

The earliest London " newspapers " were the " Corantos ", which were mainly concerned with foreign affairs.

In 1622 came a weekly pamphlet—translated from the Dutch, and issued by two London booksellers, Thomas Archer and Nicholas Bourne. Its purpose

is sufficiently indicated by the general title of the
second number, which runs :

> "The 23 of May.   Weekely Newes from Italy, Ger-
> manie, Hungaria, Bohemia, the Palatinate, France, and
> the Low Countries, Etc."

The *Weekely Newes* was the precursor of many other
similar pamphlets. These "Corantos" were followed by a series of sheets concerned with the dis-
semination of the news, dictated for the most part by
the needs of one or more of the great political parties.
When it is added that the first advertisement appeared
in the *Mercurius Britannicus* coranto on February 1,
1625, it will be seen that the modern newspaper was
already in a fair way towards establishment. It is
interesting to note that the first traders to realise the
advantage of the new method of selling their goods
were the book-sellers.

Still the slow evolution went on.   The years of the
Long Parliament saw the coming and going of many
news-sheets, *Mercury* and *Diurnal* being the titles
generally preferred.

Unfortunately the reputation of the writers of the
various pamphlets did not progress so rapidly as the
popularity of the institution they were seeking to
found.   "Liar" was the term ordinarily applied to
the newspaper writer. When a critic permitted
himself a little more latitude, the results were startling.
Here is the view of a Royalist upon the Press of the
day :

" They call him a Mercury, but he becomes the Epithet like a little negro mounted on the elephant, just such another blot rampant. He defames a good title as much as most of our modern noblemen, those Wens of greatness, the body politic's most peccant humours blistered into Lords. To call him an historian is to knight a mandrake, 'tis to view him through a perspective, and by that glass hyperbole to give the reputation of an engineer to a maker of mouse-traps."

Within one long lifetime, such as that of Hobbes, poetry and prose underwent as many radical changes as the country experienced in its political life. Take first the matter of prose.

The age now beginning was a talking age. It had changes of kings and ministers and policies to agitate it. Discoveries in natural science, proposals of social and economic theory, hazardous speculations in theology, practical and business-like topics of these kinds demanded the interest of every man and woman. The demand was followed by opportunity, by the coffee-house, the Gardens, the salons, the literary and philosophical groups formed among friends. The age talked. Because it talked about matters concerning which it had to make up its mind, it realised that earlier prose, gorgeous and involved and massive, was out of control. Therefore it set about re-fashioning it.

The need of the seventeenth century to talk, and to write its thoughts for people who were too far off to listen, explains two things. The first is the re-shaping of the language, and the second is the apparent neglect of poetry.   We shall deal with this second point more fully later.

The approach to prose may be summarised in the words by which Thomas Sprat entered the Royal Society's demand into his notes of its Proceedings—that each member should use " a close, naked, natural way of speaking; positive expressions, bringing all things as near the mathematical plainness as they can ". The syntax of the language was therefore tightened up as the century passed.   Previously it had been such that, while the great writers like Browne could scarcely fall into error, less able prose-men were little better than the writers before Fisher.   The construction of sentences held pitfalls they could find no way to avoid. Now the syntax and the very grammar are changed and fixed.   Even words are examined and defined as the first dictionary is compiled.

In this age " of prose and sense " the periodic prose of Browne or Milton is distrusted.   The brevity of Bacon is preferred as a model.   And imagination was as suspect as the musical prose of Jeremy Taylor. Imagination meant flights, which might involve loss of control.   Consequently the use of fancy must be severely restricted—a principle which affected poetry as well as prose.   In this work of many branches the first great teacher was Dryden.   Within ten years of his prefaces to his *Fables, Ancient and Modern* (1700) English prose as we know it today had been forged into a serviceable instrument.

With this accomplishment a development of prose

forms became possible, so that we come to the appearance, and some of the finest writing, of the modern essay, the rise of satirical literature not excelled since that time, and the beginning of the novel, sure of its medium and able to concentrate on perfection of structure and characterisation.

In verse the age is unique. The causes of Augustan poetry cannot recur; nothing like that poetry can come again spontaneously, either.

The earnest search for what was plain in language played no small part in making poets shun what was vague or fanciful in thought. In order to be safe, to run no risk of being caught in some metrical irregularity, it was better to be conventional and general. As a result images became standardised and the individual was discouraged. To write of a man was less correct than to " survey mankind from China to Peru ". In the end poetry became conventionalised into verse, and out of that into nonsense, as when generalisation arrived at

Innoculation ! heavenly maid ! descend . . .

These extravagances apart, there was in the eighteenth century a movement to make " numbers smooth and regular ". Human nature, city life, pastoral reflections, moral musings, were the favoured topics. The decasyllabic line in the form of the Heroic Couplet was the chosen pattern.

The movement to regularise verse had been started by Edmund Waller (he gave the honour to his predecessor, Fairfax) before the middle of the seventeenth century. Controversy broke out as to whether the couplet lines should be end-stopped—i.e. whether the sense should end with the rhyme closing each line—or whether it should ride over the rhyme into the next line. Waller end-stopped happily, so that generations of writers and readers hailed him as the first poet to regulate our verse. Dryden undid that work, which Waller himself eventually ceased to practise, although no one commented on the fact, so that the father of modern English prose gave his century a Heroic Couplet, as well as Blank Verse, free from perplexity and strongly flexible. As Pope acknowledged :

> Waller was smooth; but Dryden taught to join
> The varying verse, the full-resounding line,
> The long majestic march, and energy divine.

Incidentally, Dryden also affected the poetry of his century by determining the form of the Ode. Previously irregular, it was by him arranged into definite strophes.

Of course, there is far more in the eighteenth century than has been suggested here. When the century was less than a quarter run, new movements were stirring—movements such as the new feeling for Nature shown in Thomson's " Winter ". There was much fine song and a lyric strain not to be excelled. Our point is that the century was cast in the Augustan mould; that anything other than what was conventional, elegant, general, carefully measured, was exceptional. And it was exceptional because the main work of the century was the discovery of a language and structure and prosody which would be a reliable medium for all literary expression. The fact that the literary men who made the experiments were mostly urban in outlook and politically complacent was an added factor which tended towards the standardisation of their work. That they were also men of exceptional ability was a third element to be considered. It meant that their experiments were so successful that what they found became the canon of perfection. Thus we have the Augustan Age, when much was not Augustan and was ineffective for a time. Eventually the Romantic Revival came, to many unwelcome and unexpected. To us, however, who can look back to see why the work of the Augustans, which determined a great deal of what has become part of our prose and verse, could be no more than a phase of development, its passing is by no means surprising. Our wonder is that it lasted as long as it did. And by that wonder we show our ignorance of the bewilderment of writers and readers at the end of the seventeenth century, whose ears had been tricked by so many forms and conceits and devices that the order of Dryden and Pope and their school was a sweetness beyond all else pleasing.

The eighteenth century, then, was the time when our prose was fashioned. Yet it was far more than an age of prose, for it was a resting-place in which poets might submit to the discipline of metrical regularity, enjoy themselves in dealing with conventional themes, and be ready for the time when fresh inspiration would enable them, by the aid of a prosody clear in principles and adaptable to many forms, to enter a new age of poetry, fresh or colourful or imaginative or homely or metaphysical.

Chapter Two

Poetry—Dryden to Prior

(i) John Dryden

" EVERY age has a kind of universal genius ", and perhaps in no poet are his own words more truly verified than are those of John Dryden.

Born in 1631, in the little village of Aldwinkle in Northamptonshire, he was the son of a rector, the Rev. Erasmus Dryden, and Mary Pickering, his wife, both of whom belonged to old county families with strong Puritanical tendencies.

On leaving Cambridge in 1657, he came to London as secretary to Sir Gilbert Pickering, a kinsman of his mother and chamberlain to Oliver Cromwell. We may imagine that the young man was glad of the opportunity to add something to the small income of £40 a year which came to him on the death of his father three years earlier. His marriage in 1663 to Lady Elizabeth Howard, daughter of the Earl of Berkshire, brought another £100 a year to the family exchequer, but not a corresponding amount of happiness, since the Lady Elizabeth lacked that strong and purposeful character so marked in her husband.

Up to this time Dryden had done little to establish the great reputation that was subsequently to be his.

He had written some purely official verses in 1659, on the death of the Protector, which contrast oddly with his eulogy of Charles II on his coronation, in *Astræa Redux*, the following year. His best efforts are shown unmistakably in his early verses addressed to Dr. Charlton in 1663.

From 1663 to 1681 Dryden courted the dramatic muse; he knew his genius was not towards the drama, but it was the most lucrative branch of the literary profession at that time and he essayed it, not always with success.

His first effort, *The Wild Gallant* (1663), was a failure. Dryden himself confessed that, having made the town his judges, " the greater part condemned it ".

The Rival Ladies (1664) was more successful; but *The Indian Emperor* in 1667 established his reputation as a playwright. About twenty plays came from his pen, all more or less coarse.

The *Œdipus* (1679), written in collaboration with Nathaniel Lee, gave rise some years later to one of Dryden's trenchant remarks to a cynical acquaintance who said that it was " easy enough to write like a madman ". " No," remarked Dryden, " it is hard enough to write like a madman, but easy enough to write like a fool."

In 1665, while the Great Plague was raging, Dryden thought well to give London a wide berth, and retired to his father-in-law's house at Charlton with his wife. Here he wrote his first poem, *Annus Mirabilis* (1667), which he chose to write, as he explained to Sir Robert

Howard, " in quatrains or stanzas of four in
rhyme, because I have ever judged them mo
and of greater dignity, both for sound and i
than any other verse in use amongst us ". This poem,
dealing with the Great Fire and the war with Holland,
was dedicated to the City of London.

Two years later appeared the critical *Essay on
Dramatic Poesy*, a prose work written in the form of
a dialogue, and in 1670 the first political recognition
of his work came to him when he was asked to accept
the appointments of Poet Laureate and Historiographer
Royal, with their accompanying salaries of £200 a
year.

Jealousy soon sprang up among the literary men
of the day at the public notice taken of Dryden and
his work, and the following year George Villiers,
Duke of Buckingham, in company with Samuel
Butler, Sprat, and others, produced *The Rehearsal*,
that celebrated satire on the heroics of the existing
drama, making a special point of ridiculing Dryden.
However, the poet could afford to wait, so he took no
notice of this insult at the time; he could see the
trend of political affairs and wisely waited his opportunity. Later, when the Earl of Shaftesbury was
scheming to secure the succession of the Duke of
Monmouth, Dryden took advantage of the political
struggle between Shaftesbury and the Crown to write
his brilliant satire *Absalom and Achitophel*, in which
the King, Shaftesbury, Monmouth, and Buckingham
were all attacked.

The acquittal of Shaftesbury, on the charge of high treason preferred against him, was made the occasion of issuing a medal to commemorate the event. Dryden also commemorated it by another *Medal* (1682), a brilliant piece of satirical work.

The jealousy of his literary rivals took the form of violent abuse and caricatures of Dryden's works; Elkanah Settle wrote an amusing parody, *Absalom and Achitophel Transposed*, which was of no moment compared to the brutal and repulsive attack made in *The Medal of John Bayes*, written by Shadwell, who was the principal poet of the Whig party. This naturally provoked bitter enmity between the rival poets, and Dryden fully revenged himself by the publication of *MacFlecknoe* in October 1682 (the model of Pope's *Dunciad*), that gave Dryden's enemies an unenviable reputation for some considerable time.

Change in his religion inspired his next work, *The Hind and the Panther, a Defence of the Roman Church* (1687), which, if it accorded the poet some fame, brought him no pecuniary gain from its publication.

The following year, when William and Mary came to the throne and Protestantism was in the ascendant, Dryden fell on evil days; the salaries accompanying his public appointments were withdrawn and, worst of all, he had the chagrin of seeing Shadwell appointed to the Laureateship that had been his for eighteen years.

A feeling which arose about this time for the study of classical literature in translation inspired him to undertake several from the Latin of Juvenal and

Perseus, and his *Virgil*, published in 1697, opened up a new source of income which he did not live long to enjoy.

Of the *Ode on St. Cecilia's Day*, written three years before his death, there is given by a contemporary a striking instance of the vitality of the man. Lord Bolingbroke, a great admirer of the poet, was paying him a morning visit and, finding him unusually agitated, inquired the cause. " I have been up all the night," replied Dryden. " My musical friends made me promise to write them an ode for the feast of St. Cecilia; I have been so struck with the subject which occurred to me, that I could not leave it till I had completed it; here it is, finished at one sitting."

The Fables, his last work, a collection adapted from the works of Chaucer and Boccaccio, was published the year he died, in 1700.

His Writings

Dryden's literary significance is threefold, and is expressed in his prose, his drama, and his verse. In this section we deal exclusively with Dryden the poet.

He did not start movements; but he had a singular power of taking advantage of movement and of stamping his vigorous and keen intellect upon experimental forms which lesser and more courageous men had initiated.

The change from the romantic to the classical manner was already in evidence before Dryden was born. Dryden saw which way the wind was blowing and set his craft cheerfully in the same direction. Waller already had done creditable things with the couplet. Dryden gauged its possibilities and did brilliant things. He saw what kind of verse the people of his day wanted and made it his business to give it to them. A study of his plays shows that he was developing the qualities of ease, flexibility, and lucidity which he brought into English verse, particularly in satirical writing.

Then, at the age of fifty, after a prosperous career as a serious poet and a dramatist, he suddenly became famous in the direction where, after all, lies his especial claim on future generations—the field of satire.

His four remarkable satires were fired off in rapid succession. The first part of *Absalom and Achitophel*, directed against Shaftesbury, in 1681; *The Medal*, dealing also with Shaftesbury, 1682; *MacFlecknoe*, aimed at the Whig poet Shadwell, later in 1682; and some weeks later the second part of *Absalom and Achitophel*. Of these the finest is the Absalom (Monmouth) and Achitophel (Shaftesbury) satire, Part I.

English poetical life is pictured in a vigorous and keen manner, very little disguised by its slight Hebrew setting. The Whig leaders of the day are satirised freely and trenchantly, Monmouth alone (for Court reasons) being treated in friendly fashion. Some of the portraits are etched in with remarkable precision and point. Never before had the Heroic Couplet been used with such telling effect.

In *The Medal* we miss the tart flavour of the personalities that give piquancy to the earlier work.

The religious controversies of the time, the disputes between the Catholics and the Anglicans, and the fierce dissensions of the Nonconformists, are depicted in *Religio Laici* (1683), an argumentative poem coloured by Catholic sympathies; and *The Hind and the Panther* (1687), a clever and curious piece of work, with a very elaborate allegorical framework—the Panther being the English Church and the Hind the Church of Rome. The Presbyterian fared the worst in the poem, described as a wolf, " belly gaunt, and famished face ".

With the coming of the Revolution in 1688 the taste for classical literature became even more pronounced than heretofore. Dryden, with his sensitive finger on the public pulse, fell in with the fashion, and did a great deal of translation work from the Latin and Greek poets. The most remarkable of these was his translation of Virgil, which occupied three years, being published in 1697.

The grace and finish of the original were qualities Dryden was not competent to impart, but his splendid force and vigour give power and colour to many passages.

Already he had written an *Ode on St. Cecilia's Day*, and once again that festival inspired him to another ingenious effort—*Alexander's Feast*, on the power of music (1697). It is hard to find a more suitable description of these poems than is conveyed by the

term " ingenious ".   Clever and skilful they certainly
were, yet the attempt made to wed music and poetry
in the lines cannot be called successful.   It demanded
the lyric faculty of a Shelley or a Swinburne.   Perhaps
Swinburne alone of all our poets has had the power to
make one art the medium of conveying the æsthetic
content of another.

As a lyric-writer, he is judged better by the songs
with which his plays are interspersed and a number of
hymns that are attributed to him.   As compared
with the great lyric-writers of the previous age,
Dryden must occupy a modest place in the second
rank.

Significance and Trend of his Poetic Work.

At the end of his life Dryden described himself as one
" who had done his best to improve the language, and
especially the poetry " of his country.   To a considerable extent he was justified in saying this; for, even
putting aside his really great activities in English
prose, he had clarified and freshened English verse,
brushing away much of the picturesque yet confusing
tangle of ornamental undergrowth, and given it
point and actuality.

His dramatic verse at its best is eloquent and spirited;
his non-dramatic verse extraordinarily varied.   If
not achieving special excellence in his lyrics or his
narrative verse, he is rarely banal, always easy and
dexterous, whilst in didactic verse he is a master.   He
raised it from an indifferent form of workmanship

into the front rank and, whether in long flights, as in *Absalom and Achitophel*, or in the shorter flights, illustrated in his Prologues, Epilogues, and Fables, he is amazingly alive and original. The term " original " as applied to Dryden needs this qualification. In the sense in which it is applied to the creative shapings of high imagination, Dryden was not original. In other words, originality of " conception " is not his. But in the matter of " treatment " he is uniformly original. He invented nothing, but the crude inventions of other men he perfected, and what he said of his countrymen might well be applied to himself. " The genius of our countrymen (is) rather to improve an invention than to invent themselves."

Absalom and Achitophel

Great wits are sure to madness near allied,
And thin partitions do their bounds divide;
Else, why should he, with wealth and honour blest,
Refuse his age the needful hours of rest ?
Punish a body which he could not please,
Bankrupt of life, yet prodigal of ease ?
And all to leave what with his toil he won
To that unfeathered two-legged thing, a son,
Got, while his soul did huddled notions try,
And born a shapeless lump, like anarchy,
In friendship false, implacable in hate,
Resolved to ruin or to rule the state;
To compass this the triple bond he broke,
The pillars of the public safety shook,
And fitted Israel for a foreign yoke;
Then, seized with fear, yet still affecting fame,
Usurped a patriot's all-atoning name.

So easy still it proves in factious times
With public zeal to cancel private crimes,
How safe is treason and how sacred ill,
Where none can sin against the people's will,
Where crowds can wink and no offence be known,
Since in another's guilt they find their own !

(ii) Lesser Poets

Contemporary with Dryden was Samuel Butler, his senior by twenty years, and who died just twenty years before him.   On the Restoration, as secretary to the Lord President of Wales, he was appointed Steward of Ludlow Castle (1660), and about this time married Mrs. Herbert, a widow who was possessed of a small fortune.

During these years he had made the acquaintance of all the prominent men of his day, most of whom he satirised in his famous *Hudibras*, the first part of which was published in 1663, the second in 1664, and the third in 1678.

Notwithstanding his popularity and influential friends, Butler died in poverty in 1680.

Butler was by temperament a lover of sober common-sense and the sworn foe of enthusiasm.   Equally with Dryden is he an expression of the new mood that had seized the nation as a whole.   Inferior to Dryden in craftsmanship and versatility, he is richer in sarcastic humour;   indeed, there is more than a touch of savagery in it;   but it is a mistake to regard it as merely spiteful fun indulged in for personal reasons.

His most important work was a long, octosyllabic poem, which we know as *Hudibras*. It was a great, savage attack upon the Parliamentary party, and pleased the fancy of the time; though some, like Pepys, who loved not the Puritan, were repelled by its sustained note of scorn.

Hudibras is in lineal descent from the comic doggerel of Skelton, who, indeed, paved the way for the Restoration satirists. None before, and few after, ever used this particular metre with such happy effect as Butler.

The name *Hudibras* comes from the *Faerie Queene*. In Butler's poem he is a blusterous, ignorant, repulsive-looking Presbyterian knight, with a squire in keeping with his master.

The poem, however, with its echoes of Rabelais and Cervantes, and its wild burlesque and preposterous buffoonery, is rich in genuine flashes of comic insight. For instance :

> He that complies against his will
> Is of his own opinion still.

Such felicitously ridiculous rhymes as " duty " for " shoe-tie " give effect and variety to the monotony of the metre; and in this respect Byron and Calverley owe no small debt to him.

Limited in his gifts and certainly not squeamish in his methods, Butler is a remarkable figure in the poetic development of his time, and is one of our best exponents of satirical verse.

Hudibras

Friend Ralph, thou hast
Outrun the constable at last.
Some force whole regions, in despite
O' geography, to change their site;
Make former times shake hand with latter,
And that which was before, come after;
But those who write in rhyme still make
The one verse for the other's sake;
For one for sense, and one for rhyme,
I think's sufficient at one time,

. . . .

Doubtless the pleasure is as great
Of being cheated, as to cheat.

. . . .

With crosses, relics, crucifixes,
Beads, pictures, rosaries and pixes;
The tools of working out salvation
By mere mechanic operation.

The social condition of Restoration life, its artificial gaiety, the growing importance of London as a pleasure resort for the courtier poet, the increasing vogue of the coffee-house and the park, to which reference has been made in our introductory sketch, the growth of the political pamphlet and the journal— all these things favoured the development of satirical verse.

To the social conditions may be added also the classical taste of the day, favouring a type of literature which should be clear, concise, and topical above all things. Sir John Denham dealt with the politics of the hour in his four *Instructions to a Puritan*; Andrew Marvell, a much greater literary figure and a lyrist of sweetness and power, fell in with the fashion, and was astonishingly successful in his *Last Instructions to a Puritan*; *Advice to a Painter*; and *Britannia and Raleigh*.

John Oldham, a more powerful satirist than either of the others, wrote an ironical poem *Satire against Virtue* and was even more successful in his *Satire upon a Woman who by her falsehood and scorn was the death of my friend*. His last work was his *Satire upon the Jesuits*, perhaps the richest and most telling of his poems.

Oldham is less of the pamphleteer in verse than Marvell or Denham; he takes his subject far more seriously, as a literary artist. But he has neither Dryden's masterly technique nor Butler's ingenious humour. He writes persistently with the loud pedal on; and some of his work is like a prolonged hoarse scream.

The ballad was a popular vehicle for satire, and was in great request in town and country taverns, while literary art is at its lowest here. The humour is rough and ready, and scurrility seems to be the chief thing aimed at. To these ballads were fitted well-known tunes that had already caught the public ear in opera and play. Among such tunes the litany was a favourite, with its three lines of verse and " Libera nos, Domine " refrain. Another tune boasted the catch-phrase, " Hey boys, up we go ", which occurred about the end of the eighth line. Among the known ballad composers of the time (many ballads were anonymous, for obvious reasons), Purcell was the most famous. In general popularity Thomas D'Urfey, courtier and playwright, with his *Now the Fight's done, Sammy will never be my love again*, was no doubt his superior. But Purcell's *Lilli burlero* achieved a fame accorded to no similar effusion. It conferred distinction on Thomas, Lord Wharton's doggerel stuff, and was used afterwards again and again for still worse matter.

With the coming of Pope a new school of satire arose, lighter than the older one and, if less sincere in some respects, certainly more agreeable. Of this something will be said in a later chapter.

(iii) Court Poets of the Restoration

The drama, when it recovered from the crushing blow dealt it by Puritanism, used all its resources to lampoon its late enemy. Similarly in the Court poetry of the Restoration we may trace the violent Puritan reaction of the time.

Satire, as we shall see, usurped the place once taken by the descriptive verse of Spenser and his school; the political squib displaced the amorous sonnet, and although the lyric could still claim votaries it shared in the general change of atmosphere. Wit was esteemed above fervency; salacity above fantasy; for the song-writer was no longer, save rarely, a man of adventurous life, with a deep vein of seriousness in his nature, but a gay, irresponsible, and flippant courtier. " Every Fop wrote songs," said Sedley, one of the most brilliant of the verse-writers. The fop element was certainly very obvious in the lyric-making, for no longer did the poet rely on masculine virtues and woo his lady with hints of prowess. He wooed as did Grammont, with "pocket-looking-glass . . . essences and other small wares of love".

Among these triflers in song the names of Rochester, Buckhurst, and Sedley are conspicuous; but, unlike many of their fellows, they were men of action as well as men of letters, with deeds of daring to their credit.

John Wilmot, Earl of Rochester, is the most interesting personality of this band. Born in 1647 near Woodstock, he had a good education and proved an exceedingly apt scholar. After the usual travels, he returned to Court an accomplished personage, with abundant personal charm and still more abundant impudence.

The nearest approach to genuine feeling in this little coterie is made by this writer in some of his lyrics; as for instance, *I Cannot Change as Others do*; but the mood of mockery somehow suits him better, and many will prefer such songs as *Love and Life* with its delightful finish :

> Then talk not of inconstancy,
> False hearts and broken vows,
> If I by miracle can be,
> This livelong minute true to thee
> 'Twas all that Heav'n allows.

Scarcely inferior to him in wit and accomplishment, though less versatile as a personality, is Sir Charles Sedley.

Although he essays various forms of poetry, he is

essentially a song-writer. Less careful than Rochester in his art, he has a happy knack of agreeable song, as is proved by the well-known *Phyllis is my Only Joy*.

Lord Buckhurst (Earl of Dorset) was largely esteemed by his contemporaries, but to us today he seems on a decidedly lower level than either Rochester or Sedley—as surely as his character ranks above theirs.

His most attractive song is the familiar ditty, *To all you Ladies now on Land*, written at sea, in the first Dutch War, says the poet gravely. The specific statement may be valued in the same way as we value Defoe's *Memoirs of a Cavalier*.

(iv) Alexander Pope

The influence of the French literature of the day, considerable in Dryden's time, became even more marked in the age of his successor—Pope. This meant that increasing attention would be given to lucidity of expression and elegance of form.

Literature had now become quite frankly a literature of the Town; we can tell, even more accurately than in Shakespeare's age, the manners of the day, for in Pope's own verse the social life of the time is reflected as in a *camera obscura*. We wander in the pleasure-gardens where " quality " caroused and flirted; we note the frivolous ritual of the boudoir, hear the tapping of the inevitable snuff-box from gallants resplendent in lace ruffles; we learn the drab story of Grub Street and its denizens, the jealousies and bickerings of authors; and throughout it all there sounds the smug, complacent Deism which was as much a fashion of the time as the fluttering fans of the ladies.

At the house of a linen-draper in Lombard Street was born, in 1688, a sickly and delicate child—Alexander Pope. His talent was of the precocious order; fashioned for a life of study, he knew no other pleasure than that which comes from poring over books. Epics and tragedies he knocks off readily while in his early 'teens, and throughout his youth he reads, reads, reads—until almost he dies of overmuch study.

His great search is not the search of Paracelsus for truth; it is for style. Wycherley, now in his old age, acts as a mentor to the ambitious young man; Pope smarts under his frank criticism, and finally breaks with him.

But his promise has attracted Dryden—and when, yet on the threshold of manhood, he completed his *Essay on Criticism*, the reading public felt that a new star had arrived. What kind of radiance the star would shed was another matter.

In appearance he was singularly unimpressive.

A body of miserable weakness was a heritage from birth—headaches from his mother and a crooked figure from his father. In a moment of bitter insight, Pope once spoke of " that long disease, my life ".

By middle life Pope's physical weakness was so constant that he could not dress without aid. Cold affected him so greatly that he was compelled to wear a fur doublet under his coarse linen shirt.

> "When he rose [writes Johnson] he was invested in boddices made of stiff canvas, being scarcely able to hold himself erect until they were laced, and he then put on a flannel waistcoat. One side was contracted. His legs were so slender that he enlarged their bulk with three pairs of stockings, which were drawn on and off by the maid."

Nor did disabilities end here. He came of Catholic stock in days when English Catholics were condemned to pay double taxation. His father was no more than a minor London merchant. The boy's education was of the most miscellaneous description.

What fate did not deny to the man, Alexander Pope, was an all-dominating love for the craft of poetry. According to the light which was given him, Pope was never content with less than the polished best.

His earliest work, a set of pastorals, was quite in the fashion of the day, with the various conventional Strephons and Daphnes and orthodox pagan deities in an English religious setting of the most artificial type. The verse is uninspired but carefully modulated. In his next publication, the *Essay on Criticism*, he found himself, his public, and fame. This was followed in 1712 by *The Rape of the Lock*. The artificial tone of the age, the frivolous aspect of femininity, are nowhere more exquisitely pictured than in this poem. It is the epic of triflings; a page torn from the petty, pleasure-seeking life of a fashionable beauty; the *mise-en-scène* is the toilet chamber and the card-table.

From *The Rape of the Lock* to *Windsor Forest* is from Pope at his happiest to Pope at his worst. Pope's rhapsody on scenic charm is a melancholy thing. Far more interesting is his translation of the *Iliad* of Homer.

Quite apart from its literary merits, this translation, the fruit of ten years' arduous labour, is one of remarkable achievement for one of Pope's delicate health and limited knowledge of Greek. Bentley's caustic criticism of it as " a very pretty poem, Mr. Pope, but not Homer ", is one hard to traverse, for the Homeric breadth and vigour were ill-suited to the fastidious niceties of Pope's muse, but this has never militated against its popular success. For " a pretty poem " it certainly is, rich in felicities of the eighteenth-century pattern.

The *Iliad* was published in six volumes, for which Lintot, the publisher, paid £200 a volume, in addition to furnishing a large number of free copies for the subscribers. The *Odyssey* brought Pope in £3500, after considerable sums had been paid to assistants.

By the year 1718 Pope was in a position of independence and was able to take the house at Twickenham which is always closely associated with his memory. Both by road and river it was within easy reach of London. The poet's friends could readily come down for a chat. The plot of land around the house was large enough to secure absolute peace.

Within a few years the ideal of graceful symmetry, which is so characteristic alike of Pope and his age, pervaded every part of the garden. Some well-known lines by Pope himself suggest a lively picture of the place where half of the witty wisdom of the early eighteenth century was born.

> His garden next your admiration all
> On every side you look, behold the wall.
> No pleasing intricacies intervene,
> No artful wildness to perplex the scene;
> Grove nods at grove, each alley has a brother,
> And half the platform just reflects the other.

Bolingbroke sketched the first rough philosophical proposition eventually polished into the *Essay on Man*. And here it was that Pope, with only the silence for company, wove the tiny slips of paper upon which he was wont to jot his disjointed ideas into an harmonious whole.

> Now backs of letters, though design'd
> For those who more will need 'em,
> Are fill'd with hints and interlin'd
> Himself will scarcely read 'em.
> Each atom by some other struck
> All turns and motions tries,
> Till in a lump together stuck
> Behold a poem rise.

Lastly, it was at Twickenham, on May 30, 1744, that the restless spirit of the poet finally quitted the world which it had never loved. The bruised body was buried in Twickenham Church. The better part of the man—his work—is with us still in the form of pithy couplets, in which Alexander Pope embodied the crystal-hard wisdom of his age, and *The Rape of the Lock*.

His Work : Influence and Significance in Literature

The three poems in which Pope is emphatically the spokesman of his age are *The Rape of the Lock*, picturing its frivolities; the *Dunciad*, unveiling its squalor; the *Essay on Man*, echoing its philosophy. His own attitude towards literature is nicely expressed in the *Essay on Criticism*, where the merits and limitations of the eighteenth-century school of poetry are clearly exhibited. What they admire, what they dislike, is patent to the most casual reader. The neatness of his rapier wit is happily shown in the passing allusion to the churlish old critic John Dennis (1657–1734), author of a tragedy, *Appius and Virginia*:

But Appius reddens at each word you speak.

Of his work as a whole it may be said that he was a master of literary mosaic. There is nothing of the easy breadth and vigour of Dryden in his satirical verse; on the other hand, he excelled his predecessor in exquisite finish and detailed touches. His poems have no solidarity or homogeneity, with the exception, perhaps, of *The Rape of the Lock*. Rather may they be likened to polished fragments, cunningly fitted to form a whole and remarkable for workmanship rather than integral beauty.

Using the Drydenian couplet, he imparted to it a gossamer-like delicacy of touch that more than compensated for the lack of strength. If at times the glitter and sparkle faded into dullness, the occasions are comparatively rare, and the amazing thing is that he sustained his mercurial smartness and aptness for so long. There are few graces of style beyond crispness and lightness. The beauties, though abundant, are of the obvious kind; and there is no hint in his work of high imagination, of subtle fancy, no sense of mystery, no romance, no depth of feeling, no greatness of impulse.

> Avoid extremes; and shun the fault of such
> Who still are pleased too little or too much.
> At every trifle scorn to take offence,
> That always shows great pride, or little sense;
> Those heads, as stomachs, are not sure the best,
> Which nauseate all, and nothing can digest.
> Yet let not each gay turn thy rapture move;
> For fools admire, but men of sense approve;
> As things seem large which we through mists descry,
> Dullness is ever apt to magnify.
> Some foreign writers, some our own despise;
> The ancients only, or the moderns prize.
> Thus wit, like faith, by each man is applied
> To one small sect, and all are damned beside.
> Meanly they seek the blessing to confine,
> And force that sun but on a part to shine,
> Which not alone the southern wit sublimes,
> But ripens spirits in cold northern climes;
> Which from the first has shone on ages past,
> Enlightens the present, and shall warm the last;
> Though each may feel increases and decays,
> And see now clearer and now darker days.
> Regard not, then, if wit be old or new,
> But blame the false, and value still the true.[1]

[1] *Essay on Criticism.*

(v) Prior, Gay, and Others

Among minor verse writers of the age, Matthew Prior, " beloved by every Muse ", was a Dorset man, born near Wimborne in 1664, who by the generosity of an uncle was educated at Westminster School, and at St. John's College, Cambridge, under the patronage of the Earl of Dorset. During this period he collaborated with Charles Montagu, in *The Town Mouse and the City Mouse*, a burlesque on *The Hind and the Panther* of Dryden.

On leaving Cambridge several diplomatic appointments were conferred upon him, including those of Secretary of State for Ireland (1697) and Under-Secretary of State in England (1699). Two years later he was elected member for East Grinstead, at this time changing his political coat from Whig to Tory. The Tories made him Commissioner of Customs (1711–14), during which time he took some part in formulating the Peace of Utrecht, and was Queen Anne's ambassador at Paris until her death. In 1715 he was impeached and for two years imprisoned.

Having made £4000 by the publication of a folio edition of his works in 1719, Lord Harley added a similar sum in order to make some provision for Prior's old age; unfortunately, Prior lived only two years to enjoy this good fortune, dying in 1721.

Prior wrote two long poems : *Solomon on the Vanity of the World*, and *Alma, or The Progress of the Mind.*

Just as Prior wrote unsuccessful imitations of Spenser and Chaucer, so in *Alma* he imitated Butler's Hudibrastic verse. Opinion as to its value is divided, chiefly because the author put a good deal of thought and learning into a form and style essentially light.

Solomon, in three books, is more successful; it is written in the manner of Dryden, with numerous Alexandrines.

Prior lives chiefly because of his lighter, shorter poems, some of which were written for young people. His importance lies in his skilful handling of the octosyllabic couplet and, still more, in his freedom away from it. When the convention of that couplet was almost *de rigueur* in its application, Prior did not hesitate to use an anapæstic tetrameter, in which he had considerable success. This is particularly the case in the making of literary *soufflé*. No one could better fling off some audacious trifle or dainty sentimentality. The airy deftness of his touch is delicious, and deludes the reader at times into rating him merely as a light-hearted jester. Here is an example of his thought expressed in the measure which he more or less introduced into poetry.

To Chloe

What I speak, my fair Chloe, and what I write, shows
    The difference there is betwixt Nature and Art;
I court others in verse, but I love thee in prose;
    And they have my whimsies, but thou has my heart.

The god of us verse-men—you know, Child—the Sun,
  How after his journeys he sets up his rest;
If at morning o'er earth 'tis his fancy to run,
  At night he reclines on his Thetis's breast.

So when I am weary with wandering all day,
  To thee, my delight, in the evening I come;
No matter what beauties I saw in my way,
  They were but my visits, but thou art my home.

Among the minor versifiers of the time we note
Ambrose Philips, who also found favour with verses
for children, so that Carey (of *Sally in Our Alley* fame)
nicknamed him " Namby-Pamby ". The name has
stuck, not only to Philips, but to all other versifiers of
over-simplified and over-sweetened confections.

More important is John Byrom (1692–1763),
physician, Jacobite, mystic, first teacher of a reliable
system of shorthand, friend and disciple of William
Law. Byrom's habit of versifying almost anything
he wrote about makes most of his work useless. Yet
a few of his epigrams and his delightful prose *Private
Journal* will always find discerning readers. Of his
poetry, the best remembered is the hymn, " Christians,
awake ".

John Gay was born in 1685 at Barnstaple in Devon,
and lost both his parents when ten years old. Coming
of an impoverished family, he tried his fortune as
apprentice to a London silk mercer, and later on drifted
into a secretaryship to the Duchess of Monmouth.
He had a rich gift for vivid description—a rural scene

or the delights of the town, it mattered not to Gay; he could do either equally well.

Lacking the originality of Prior, he had a goodly share of humour, considerable technical skill, whether in turning out the favourite couplet of the time or evolving a lyric. Among his best works may be noted *Rural Sports*; *Trivia, or the Art of Walking the Streets of London*; the famous *Black-eyed Susan*; the equally agreeable if less well-known lyrics—*Phillida*, and *'Twas when the Seas were Roaring*, and some capital Fables.

Easy good humour marks both Prior and Gay. They are typical products of their age, genuine artists in their way; and modest as that way might be, rarely dull save when they tried to be serious.

St. Clement's

Where the fair columns of St. Clement stand,
Whose straiten'd bounds encroach upon the Strand,
Where the low penthouse bows the walker's head,
And the rough pavement wounds the yielding tread;
Where not a post protects the narrow space,
And strung in twines, combs dangle in thy face;
Summon at once thy courage, rouse thy care,
Stand firm, look back, be resolute, beware.
Forth issuing from steep lanes, the collier's steeds
Drag the black load; another cart succeeds,
Team follows team, crouds heap'd on crouds appear
And wait impatient till the road grow clear.
Now all the pavement sounds with tramping feet,
And the mixt hurry barricades the street.
Entangled here, the waggon's lengthen'd team
Cracks the tough harness; here a pond'rous team

Lies overturn'd athwart; for slaughter fed
Here lowing bullocks raise their hornèd head.
Now oathes grow loud, with coaches coaches jar,
And the smart blow provokes the sturdy war;
From the high box they wave the thong around
And with the twining lash their shins resound;
Their rage ferments, more dangerous wounds they try,
And the blood gushes down their painful eye.
And now on foot the frowning warriors light,
And with their pond'rous fists renew the fight;
Blow answers blow, their cheekes are smear'd with blood
Till down they fall, and grappling roll in mud.

. . . . .

Fair Chloe blushed; Euphelia frowned:
    I sung, and gazed; I played, and trembled:
And Venus to the Loves around
    Remarked how ill we all dissembled.

. . . . .

The fly that sips treacle is lost in the sweets.

. . . . .

    When yet was ever found a mother
    Who'd give her booby for another?

Three poets of the time stand apart from their
fellows, as marking the transitional spirit between the
school of Dryden and Pope and the Romantic movement in verse that started with Thomson's *Seasons*.
Edward Young, Thomas Parnell, and Lady Winchelsea
stood to some extent for the new spirit; in their treatment of external nature they belonged more to the
Romantic than the Critical movement.

Lady Winchelsea, for instance, was singled out for
commendation by Wordsworth because of her
Nocturnal Reverie. Parnell made a notable break away
from the eternal couplet of the time, and Young, for

all his pretentiousness, showed a gloomy gravity quite different from the easy-going sententiousness of Pope and his school.

It is probable, however, that none of these was conscious of any innovating tendencies. The difference in tone is due rather to temperamental peculiarities than to any change of literary attitude. Young in his *Universal Passion* (1725–28) proved almost as skilful a satirist as Pope himself. His most characteristic work is the *Night Thoughts*, a lengthy poem of sententious reflection, showing considerable technical skill in his management of Blank Verse, but handicapped by a stilted, theatrical phraseology.

Parnell, like Young, suffered vicissitudes and disappointments which are found reflected in his verse. More varied than Young, he achieved some excellent translations, and showed freshness and observation as well as metrical power in *The Night-piece on Death* and *Hymn to Contentment*.

Lady Winchelsea (1660–1725) was closely in touch with the literary wits of the age—indeed, she is Pope's Ardelia—and presents a curious and sometimes piquant mixture of the old and the new in her methods. While not sufficiently original to break away from the literary conventions of her time, she none the less had a more genuine feeling for nature. In some respects *The Nocturnal Reverie* is better entitled to be regarded as the pioneer of the Nature poetry of the new age than even Thomson's *Seasons*; it is less rhapsodical, less conventional in its phraseology.

It is quite evident that we have come to the parting of the ways. Before leaving it, let us recall the solid merits of the school that were undervalued and slighted rather unfairly by the brilliant critics in the Romantic period; these in particular—the finished art of its satire; the creation of a delightful type of butterfly poetry in the *vers de société*; above all, the clarity and succinctness introduced into English verse.

Chapter Three

Prose—Dryden to Evelyn

(i) Pioneers of the Essay

AMONG the great Elizabethan writers there are suggestions here and there of a plainer, simpler, more straightforward prose. Bacon in his *Essays* and Jonson in his *Discoveries* diverge certainly at times from the elaborate Elizabethan pattern, wrought to such cunning perfection by men like Browne, and Burton, and Sir Walter Raleigh.

The prose of the new age is far better adapted to an age richer in political and philosophic speculation than in poetry, in the art of critical exposition and journalistic realism than in work of creative imagination.

Cowley may be regarded as the initial pioneer of the new movement. He is a pioneer by no means certain of his medium, nor even constant to it; yet in both his essays and his *Discourse concerning the Government of Oliver Cromwell* (1661) the change of literary attitude is apparent.

Once regarded as the greatest poet of his day, Cowley is now chiefly remembered for his little essays, in *Several Discourses by way of Essays*. As in his poetry, but with consequences here less harmful to his fame, Cowley embodies much of the old with what is original.

58

Unmistakably new in prose are his colour and fire, and a lightness of touch which he may have gained during his sojourn in Paris at the time of the Civil War.

Dryden's importance as a prose-writer derives from his ease, his force, his intellectual vigour, which were specially serviceable when prose had suffered from over-riotous living.

Apart from its brilliant analysis of dramatic principles, his *Essay on Dramatic Poesy* (1668) is a model of the new prose. Probably Corneille was the dominant influence in its formation; some have seen in later work the effects of Montaigne. Certainly Dryden did much to stimulate interest in the essay as a form. Dryden's prose is nearly always strong, flexible, and delightfully straightforward.

Sir William Temple, son of Sir John Temple, Master of the Rolls in Ireland, was born in 1628, educated at Cambridge, and became a member of the Irish Parliament in 1660.

His " Essays " on various subjects—Health, Gout, Gardening, and Poetry—are written in a clear, agreeable, unaffected style, rising at times to a rhythmic beauty, as in the *Essay on Poetry*. They certainly show that the ease and the intimacy of the new school need not be divorced from dignity and charm.

Temple's contemporary, Lord Halifax (George Savile), was a Yorkshireman, born at Thornhill in 1633.

Halifax was a political force as well as a man of letters and achieved fame from his pamphlet *The*

Character of a Trimmer, which indicates accurately his own political attitude; became famous as a parliamentary speaker; and in a volume of *Miscellanies* (*c.* 1688) which contained essays on various subjects, and a few notable pamphlets, showed grace, lucidity, and terseness. He writes more like the man of the world than did Temple, and his aphorisms have a pleasant, satirical flavour, as that on " An Empty Woman " : " Such a one is seldom serious but with her tailor "; or this, " You may love your children without living in the nursery ".

In all these writers the influence of Montaigne is very marked, none more so than in Halifax.

Of other famous contemporaries, forerunners of the great prose age, Tillotson and Bunyan, I speak elsewhere. Bunyan really stands by himself; there are in him no traces of foreign models and classical influences. He is the chief of Puritanism, and the Bible and his own native genius are the only outstanding factors. That is why he was treated in the last phase of the Renascence rather than in the first phase of classical reaction.

(ii) The Great Essayists

Long after feudalism had perished as a political force, it lingered on as a social and literary influence. Intensely individualistic as was the spirit of the Renascence, it left many old customs untouched by its anti-feudal tendencies. Sentiment of the Restoration favoured the continuance and vitality of these survivals—ancient habits of thought and life. So, looking at the life of the period, we detect two contrary currents of opinion, the one fed by Puritanism, the other by feudalism. The best instincts of the nation had recoiled alike from the narrow rigidity of the Puritan ideal and the shallow self-indulgence of the Restoration hedonists. In religious matters they had found a *via media*; they now sought one in their social and political life. In this work of reconciliation it is hard to over-estimate the influence of Joseph Addison (1672–1719).

The star of Congreve was rising, that of Dryden declining; and Congreve, it is said, introduced Addison to Montague, Chancellor of the Exchequer. Addison wrote a poem to the King in 1695, and dedicated a Latin poem on the Peace of Ryswick (1697) to Montague himself.

Pope had declared that Addison spent much of his time at coffee-houses with his friends, a habit which Pope himself found injurious to health. It is probable that Addison's social proclivities led him into the habit of intemperance which possibly shortened his life. But there is no doubt that " Canary wine and Barbadoes water " frequently unlocked a flood of rich eloquence and fine suggestion. One recalls the witty saying of Coleridge, that " some men are like musical glasses; you only get the finest tones from them when they are wet ".

Pope was an excellent talker; scarcely an effective conversationalist. He belonged to the genus of

Coleridge and Carlyle rather than to that of Hazlitt and Macaulay.

Steele and Addison were educated at the same school and were friends at Oxford. But while Addison shaped as the " good little boy ", Steele's career suggested a collegiate Harry Sandford.

In April 1709 Steele started *The Tatler*. Addison contributed a few papers to the earlier numbers, but not till the eighty-first number did he become a frequent contributor.

The *Tatler* started by detailing news mingled with essays and stories and dramatic criticism. It was through the influence of Addison that the essay became the most important constituent.

January 2, 1711, saw the death of the *Tatler*, and the following March 1 the birth of *The Spectator*. It ran for 555 numbers, continuing until December 6, 1712. The essay which had proved so great a success in the *Tatler* became the one ingredient in the *Spectator*. The sobriety and moderation displayed by the writers, the humour, the genial moralising—these qualities made for the stupendous success of the journal. It has been well said that " the *Spectator* made a mark in English literature, and fixed a form that was adopted with servile fidelity by many periodicals to the end of the century ".

In his supreme characterisation—the mellow Sir Roger de Coverley—all that is finest in the old feudalism finds expression.

Steele sketches him in the second *Spectator*; but he

is more richly embroidered in the fifteenth *Spectator* by Addison, where Sir Roger is introduced in his own country house.

After journalism came playwriting. *Cato* was produced at Drury Lane and, despite its dramatic tameness, scored a great success. Pope had written an elegant prologue for it, and Swift, it is said, attended one of the rehearsals.

Then came another period of essay-writing, this time for the *Guardian*, the successor to the *Spectator*.

The character and genius of Addison are best exemplified in the pages of the *Spectator*. It is hard to better the comment that he " may be said to have almost created and wholly perfected English prose as an instrument for the expression of social thought ". If we compare Addison's prose with the prose of Milton or Hooker or Bacon, we shall realise the de-lightful plasticity, the delightful " nuances " of mood and fancy, for which Addison finds expression. The earlier stylists were rich in eloquence and in the gift of noble declamation; but they speak in full dress from, as it were, a rostrum. In the *Tatler* and *Spectator* we have the beginning of that genial intimacy of the writer with the reader which was to find so rare a following at a later time in Elia, in Hazlitt, and in Thackeray.

With all this flexibility and ease there is no slipshod writing. So fastidious in his workmanship that, according to Warton, he would stop the press on occasion to alter a preposition or conjunction. Thus for the manner. For the matter, the happy blend of the Puritan spirit and the Renascence spirit proved greatly to the taste of his countrymen. " I have," he said truly enough, " brought philosophy out of closets and libraries, schools and colleges, to dwell at clubs and assemblies, at tea-tables and in coffee-houses."

The *Spectator* was probably a picture of Addison himself. He is a gentleman who, after studying soberly and well at the University, betakes himself to London, and there notes all the phases of life to be observed; he listens to the wits at Wills's, smokes with " the philosopher of the Grecian ", maybe with the politician at the " St. James's ", and with the merchants at the " Exchange ".

The trend of the essays in the *Spectator* is thus characterised by the author: " The great and only end of these speculations is to banish vice and ignorance out of the territories of Great Britain."

From the outset Addison's face is set against the shameless licence and shallowness of Restoration manners; he attacks the fashionable youths and cynical men about town who are " knight-errants " of vice. To him they are " a sort of vermin ". When he wishes he can smite hard; but his favourite mood is a mood of delicate and playful satire, and here he is at his happiest. Swift is his superior at the sledgehammer work.

Of Addison's verse there is less to say. There is little here that has survived the exacting criticism of posterity. His plays have no lasting quality. Neither he nor Steele had the dramatic gift. Sentiment and humour there are—especially in the opera of *Rosamond* (1707), but his faculty of characterisation, so happily displayed in the essays, finds no congenial outlook in terms of the theatre. *Cato*, celebrated in his day, is one of the dullest plays ever written by a great author.

Richard Steele (1672–1729). Genial, impulsive, good-natured, improvident " Dick " Steele was the son of a Dublin attorney who died when his son was five years old.

Without counting the cost, Steele always did that which appealed most strongly to his own inclination. The Battle of the Boyne was in the air and the fever of war fired his blood. Failing to obtain a commission in the army, he enlisted as a private in the Coldstream Guards, to the disgust of his uncle, who disinherited him. He, however, soon rose from the ranks and became the favourite and secretary of his colonel, Lord Cutts, to whom he dedicated *The Procession* (1695), some elegiac verses written on the death of Queen Mary.

In 1701 he wrote *The Christian Hero*. The following year, as a counterblast to this sermon, appeared *The Funeral*; in 1704 *The Lying Lover*, which Steele said was " damned for its piety "; *The Tender Husband* in 1703, and after a lapse of seventeen years, *The Conscious Lovers*, in which Mrs. Oldfield and Colley Cibber took parts.

In 1707 Steele was appointed editor to the official

organ of the Government, *The London Gazette*. In 1709, as we have seen, he started the *Tatler*, and later the *Spectator* and the *Guardian*, all of which added to his fame as an essayist.

Steele's journalistic work on the *Tatler* and *Spectator* has already been discussed when dealing with Addison. He was too conscientious a moralist in his writing to be a playwright, and his attempt to redeem the drama from the grossness and licence of the Restoration stage led him into many sentimental ineptitudes. There is more vitality in his plays than in those of Addison, but he has no sense of construction.

Addison and Steele were admirably suited as co-craftsmen, for each could give what the other lacked. Steele brought to his work a wide experience of life, generous sympathies, and a sunny humour; Addison brought a wide experience of literature, a polished style, and just a pleasant tang of acidity in his humour. Both were moralists at heart, with much the same outlook on the society of their day.

Daniel Defoe (1661?–1731).   To many people Defoe is chiefly known as the author of *Robinson Crusoe* (1719) and a few other tales dealing with low life. Yet fiction was merely an incident in Defoe's astoundingly varied career. He was fifty-eight when he wrote *Robinson Crusoe* and before that time he had been a merchant, a manufacturer, a satirist, a public official, and an editor.

Defoe was born in London at St. Giles', Cripplegate (*c.* 1660–1).

His first known pamphlet was written in verse, and published during the Revolution of 1688. Here he declares he had never written before and would never write again unless his pamphlet took effect.

Everything that Defoe says about himself must be taken with reservation and, when possible, substantiated elsewhere, for from his earliest years he was constitutionally unable to tell the truth, and even his name is an experiment in fiction, his father's name being Foe.

He served William III in good stead by his pamphlet in defence of a standing army and by some ingenious lines on *The True-born Englishman*. These verses, coming at a time when popular feeling was against the King and his Dutch followers, are a tribute to Defoe's courage.

With William's death in 1702 Defoe's era of prosperity closed. Under Anne the High Church party became dominant, and bitterness towards Dissenters was the order of the day. This evoked one of the most remarkable of Defoe's pamphlets, and one that established him beyond doubt as an artist in fiction. In 1702 appeared anonymously *The Shortest Way with the Dissenters*, in which, with ironic skill, he reduced to absurdity the High Church position. Unhappily, the irony was too subtle to be appreciated, and both Churchmen and Dissenters were furious. To use his own words, " The world flew at him like a dog with a broom at his tail ".

He was tried, found guilty of seditious libel, fined, and subjected to the pillory.

He stood before the Royal Exchange in Cornhill, on the last three days of July 1703; but had no bad time of it, for admirers clustered round and threw flowers in place of garbage, since he was a popular favourite.

In 1704 there emanated from Newgate the first number of a *Review* written by Defoe. It was a political newspaper.

In this paper he showed, moreover, some of the qualities of Cobbett: incision and independence, and a command of vigorous, flexible English.

But he was not really an independent critic. He could not afford to be. The Government, he knew, would pounce down on him at the first attack on them. So on some matters he was "reticent", as he afterwards explained, distinguishing between reticence and falsehood.

In July 1706 appeared *The True Relation of the Apparition of one Mrs. Veal*, that gave further proof of his power to create that illusion of truth which is the very life force of fiction.

When Godolphin was dismissed and Harley came back to office, the *Review* changed politics. This is one of the evils of "patronage". Defoe was not squeamish, being neither better nor worse than the majority of his day. In his heart Defoe was Whig and, when he could do so safely, he served the Whigs with his pen.

About 1718 politics became more humdrum and Defoe, after another visit to prison (for libel), looked for fresh worlds to conquer.

On April 25, 1719, appeared the first volume of *Robinson Crusoe*, founded on the four years' residence of Alexander Selkirk in the Island of Juan Fernandez. Captain Roger, who released Selkirk, had told the story; so also had Steele in the *Englishman*.

Defoe sold his book to William Taylor, a publisher, who made a fortune by it. Owing to its enormous success, a second volume was written, and a book of *Crusoe's Serious Reflections* followed.

Then came *Captain Singleton* (1720), *Moll Flanders* (1721), *Colonel Jacque* (1722), *Journal of the Plague Year* (1722), *Roxana* (1724), *A Tour through Great Britain* (1724-26), *A New Voyage Round the World* (1725), *The Political History of the Devil* (1726), *The Complete English Tradesman* (1725-27), *System of Magic* (1726), and the *Essay on the Reality of Apparitions* (1727).

During his later years Defoe lived at Stoke Newington, with stables and pleasure-grounds, and kept a coach.

The last few years of Defoe's life are enveloped in some mystery. He was writing a book—*The Complete English Gentleman*—when he broke it off in September 1729 and fled. Why, is not clear. He never returned home, but died in 1731 at a lodging in Moorfields; possibly the avoidance of his creditors in the interest of his family was the reason for his disappearance; anyhow, he did not die in distress;

and his affection for his daughter is shown to the last.

(a) *His Realistic Imagination.* Defoe's imagination was realistic in the sense that it imparted to the reader the illusion of reality that the story-teller hitherto had despised. " Fact . . . I can assure you ", he is always whispering to the reader.

Everybody likes the air of verisimilitude. The novel reader asks to be " taken in ", and he likes it to be done well. Defoe managed it in style.

In short, Defoe proved himself an accomplished liar; and since all good story-telling is the art of lying brilliantly, his success as a novelist is quite comprehensible.

(b) *His Power of Detail.* The entire fascination of *Robinson Crusoe* lies in its details. Children love details. They want to know how many biscuits he ate, and how often the parrot spoke. That all this is wildly unessential does not matter. Defoe knew its effectiveness and told them.

The detail is lucidly given; it is not flung in an undigested heap at the reader; it is not oppressively technical. It is clear, orderly, and sufficient. The style of Defoe is admirably suited to this method.

Nowhere is the power of detail better used than in *The History of the Plague Year.*

Here, at the outset, is struck the note of matter-of-fact realism, and never throughout the work is the illusion removed that you are reading the strictly veracious account of an eye-witness; as, for instance, the ghastly scene in Tokenhouse Yard, Lothbury, where a woman looking out of the window " gave three frightful screeches, and then cried, ' Oh ! death, death, death ! ' in a most inimitable tone, and which struck me with horror and a chilliness in my very blood ".

(c) *His Interest in Contemporary Life*. Defoe had a thorough knowledge of men and women, not of the noblest souls, perhaps, but of good average humanity.

So he gave his public pirates and pick-pockets, and loose women, and even threw in a few backslidings in the case of Crusoe; and the public read, enjoyed, and thanked Heaven they were not as these creatures were.

Defoe might have treated the flotsam and jetsam of life very differently. He might have shed a humanitarian glow around them, as Dickens would; he might have shocked us by painting in real colours all the depravity, and hopelessness, and animalism, as Gorky would; he might have taken them with the tolerant humour and easy good-nature of Thomas Nash. But he was not built like that, and, though no doubt he could have made them much more " alive " than he did, he had to suit his public. We must not be too hard on him for that.

His interest in contemporary life made him realise exactly what the Englishman is; what his likes and dislikes are; and he reproduces these in *Crusoe*. He meets a savage and preaches at him with true missionary zeal. He carried his prejudices into other countries. They must give way to him, for he is an *Englishman*. But if he has the limitations of a Saxon, he has also finer qualities : a sense of justice, and a dislike of humbug.

What does this mean ?

It means that he eschewed the sentimental appeal; he let the facts of his story carry with them their own implication.

As a writer he helped to kill the high-falutin' romance, for long a favourite; and while his lack of imaginative depth and tenderness gave pronounced limitations to his work, and his didacticism was often oppressive, yet with obvious failings he combined considerable and often underrated merits. He was fair-minded and good-hearted—no small matter in those days—a good fighter, who fought honestly in the open; and if his ideals were not very inspiring, he never pretended they were : in short, a sincere, just, kindly, unaffected man.

Jonathan Swift (1667–1745). Of English parentage, Jonathan Swift was born in Dublin, November 30, 1667.

After a brief school career at Kilkenny, he went to Trinity College, Dublin. Coming to England, he became secretary to Sir William Temple, then living in retirement near Farnham.

Temple seems to have done all he could for the young man but was unable to secure him any definite position, beyond obtaining for him the prebend of Kilroot, near Belfast, shortly after he had taken priest's

Orders in 1694. There he stayed for two years, returning to Temple in 1696.

At Kilroot we hear of Swift's first love affair, with Miss Waring, an heiress, known to us as " Varina ", to whom he proposed by letter in 1696, a definite answer to which was left in abeyance by the lady. He, however, corresponded with her till 1700, when a final letter of Swift's, by no means to his credit, ended the matter between them.

During this time he acted as tutor to Esther Johnson, a humble dependant of Temple, a child when Swift first met her, who grew up to be a beautiful woman, destined as " Stella " to play a big part in Swift's emotional life.

Sir William Temple died in 1699, and made Swift his literary executor. Up to this time Swift had published nothing of his own work, but had "writ and burnt", as he wrote to a brother cleric, " and writ again upon all manner of subjects, more than perhaps any man in England ". *The Battle of the Books* was written in 1697 but did not appear till it was published with *The Tale of a Tub* in 1704.

The year following Temple's death Swift returned to Ireland with Lord Berkeley, then Deputy, being his secretary and chaplain; in addition to this he was also appointed to a group of small livings near Dublin that brought him an income of £200 a year.

Returning to England with Lord Berkeley in 1701, Swift was soon in the midst of a political crisis, throwing all his energies into the cause of the Whigs, and writing on their behalf his pamphlet *On the Dissensions in Athens and Rome*, notwithstanding that, as a churchman, his sympathies were on the whole more in accordance with the policy of the Tories. Neither party, however, realising his hopes, he threw up politics for the time being and in disgust returned to Ireland in 1709.

His Tory pamphlet, *The Conduct of the Allies*, appeared on November 27, 1711; a few days later a second edition was printed and sold out in a few hours, and 11,000 copies were in circulation by the end of January.

While he was in the heyday of his triumphs in political circles there was another side of the man shown to us in his *Journal to Stella*, a series of letters written to Esther Johnson, whom he had known intimately as a child.

On April 23, 1713, Swift was appointed Dean of St. Patrick's, Dublin. This was the first personal recognition of his political work, but, as it involved a payment of £1000 for a house and fees, was perhaps not so great a reward as it appeared.

Swift seems to have felt acutely the change from the rush of politics and congenial companionship to the loneliness and comparative obscurity of his life in Dublin. However this may be, Ireland was in the throes of famine and crime consequent on the passing of an Act in 1696 restricting trade with the Colonies and prohibiting the export of woollen manufactures. Swift's sense of justice rebelled at this and in 1720 he wrote the *Proposal for the Universal Use of Irish Manufactures*, wherein he begs every man and woman to make an earnest resolution " never to appear with one single shred that comes from England ". Four years later appeared the famous *Drapier Letters*, which were published anonymously; on their author's identity being disclosed, Swift became the idol of the poor in Ireland.

In 1708 Swift had made the acquaintance of " Vanessa "—Hester Vanhomrigh—an intellectual and accomplished woman whose love for him was the tragedy of her life; his rage at a letter she had written to " Stella " brought their friendship of years to an abrupt conclusion, and caused her death from grief and jealousy in 1723. Through directions in her will that Swift's poems and letters to her should be published, the poems appeared in 1726 under the title of *Cadenus and Vanessa*, but the letters were not published till after his death.

Gulliver's Travels was published in 1726. Two years later (1728) Swift's beloved " Stella " died—" the truest, most virtuous, and valuable friend that I, or any other person, was ever blessed with ".

The loss of his friend Sheridan in 1738, and the gradual passing away of all those great intellects with whom he had fraternised, combined with the shadow of insanity that was overclouding his brain, made his last years more and more lonely and helpless, and at length he lost all means of communication with the world. Death came and released him on October

19, 1745, and he lies buried with " Stella " in his own cathedral of St. Patrick's, Dublin.

" Swift was a wild beast who worried and baited all mankind almost, because his intolerable arrogance, vanity, pride, and ambition were disappointed." Thus Horace Walpole. Here is another verdict in a different key : " By far the greatest man of that time, I think, was Jonathan Swift. . . . He saw himself in a world of confusion and falsehood; no eyes were clearer to see it than his." Such are the words of Thomas Carlyle.

Some clue may be found, perhaps, if we consider what was the special quality of Swift's satire.

In certain respects Swift resembles Defoe. There is direct vigour and matter-of-factness about his satire and, like Defoe, he uses irony to drive home a point. Less wide in his range than Defoe, and more savage in his methods, he sounds profounder depths and exhibits a more cosmic humour than his contemporary. The humour is often bitter as gall, but his power and appositeness are beyond question. Tragedy is written across Swift's life. His intellectual audacity stood in his own pathway. There could be no preferment to the churchman who so mercilessly ridiculed theology in *The Tale of a Tub*; no happiness for a lover so capricious and incalculable as he; no content for a man who, in an age when the emotional life was kept so sternly subjected, looked out upon life with such fierce and passionate intensity of feeling. He is like a man born out of due time; and though he stands alone among the men of his age, unable to endure the easy cynicism of men like Gay, or to follow the genial humanity of Steele and the graceful urbanities of Addison, yet he was not great enough to rise above them. On the critical side he is supremely great; none could despise the world and mankind with such brilliant fury. But he had no alternative; nothing to put in the place of material ambition. He is at heart as worldly as Defoe; and it is part of his tragedy that he recognises the fact.

The interest of *The Battle of the Books*—Swift's first important work—for the literary student today lies entirely in the flashes of satiric fancy with which he lights up his subject. The academic controversy of modern *versus* ancient which excited so many of Swift's contemporaries seems to us both foolish and futile. The inconclusive finish to the battle is a good touch. Literary combatants are never slain.

To an extent also the musty flavour of ancient controversies pervades *The Tale of a Tub*; but the work stands on a much higher level. There is no fiercer satire in the language than this attack on the churches. Written from the point of view of an Anglican who wishes to show up the folly and wickedness of other religious communions, Swift practically riddles his own church with the shot intended only for his enemy—and the end of the onslaught sees all theologies in ruin. As an ironic exposure of human infirmities, *The Tale of a Tub* is a masterpiece, though its unrelieved cynicism makes it oppressive reading.

Swift's profound contempt for the average man is tremendous. Beside the cold fury of his sarcasm, Carlyle's dictum, "Thirty millions—mostly fools", reads like a mere flash of petulance. Swift disagreed with the Deists, who held that religion, being based on reason, would be strengthened by free inquiry. "Free inquiry!" sneered the Dean; "why, the bulk of the people are 'as well qualified for flying as for thinking.'" This is the *rationale* of Swift's religious standpoint. We need religion as the one security for social order.

No understanding of Swift's undoubted fascination for women is possible, however, without studying his *Journal to Stella* and the verses of Vanessa. The first is especially important, for it reveals, beneath the harsh violence of the man, a vein of curious tenderness and whimsicality.

Of all Swift's books, *Gulliver's Travels* (1726–27) has proved the most popular. The reason is not hard to seek, for the earlier portion appeals both to the child and to the grown-up, and the parable he tells is thrown into the form of a pseudo-realistic narrative, whose secret he had learned from Defoe. There is playfulness of fancy, a lightness of touch about the early books, a simplicity of treatment, that gives it a readier access of appeal. The later books are clouded by the insanity of Swift's last days and the pleasant fantasy degenerates into nauseous bitterness. Yet, while allowing the superior attractiveness of Gulliver, the greater originality and intellectual power of *The Tale of a Tub* are equally incontestable. That work exhibits best Swift's genius as a satirist.

As a force in letters, Swift has impressed our own time more than he did his own. No ironist save Defoe, or Fielding in *Jonathan Wild*, proved as clear and unequivocal as he; and Swift's irony, unlike theirs, glows with consuming intensity of feeling. The words are running molten lead. As other great stylists of the time—Pope and Addison—he achieves a triumphant clarity; but, unlike Pope, he is never epigrammatic; unlike Addison, he has little plasticity of form. There is no contemporary who impresses one more by his marked sincerity and concentrated passion.

Swift's chief value as a writer lies in his challenge to an easy, complacent optimism, and yet even here the man is greater than his work. He remains a tragic and sombre figure, reviling his age and crushed by it; an Ajax defying the lightning and smitten with blindness. No finer thing has been said of his tragic life than was said by Thackeray : " To think of him is like thinking of the ruin of a great Empire."

(iii) Lesser Prose-writers

Among the lesser prose-writers of the time is Dr. John Arbuthnot, the great-hearted friend of Swift.

Born in 1667, a student at Aberdeen and Oxford, Arbuthnot graduated M.D. at the Scottish university of St. Andrews. Called upon to attend Prince George of Denmark during a sudden attack of illness while at Epsom, he speedily became a favourite with the royal family and, in 1709, was appointed physician to Queen Anne. At her death came reverses which he bore with equanimity and, after twelve years of ill-health, he died in 1735. He was a noted physician, a ripe scholar, a wit who could hold his own with the best of his contemporaries, a collaborator with Pope, and the friend of John Gay.

As a writer he lacked the originality of the great prose-men; followed frankly the literary methods of Swift; avoided his bitterness, and did much to popularise his master by drawing attention to his genius.

Arbuthnot's most characteristic work is his *History of John Bull* (1712). It gives an amazing picture of the social history of the age, somewhat in the vein of Swift. More easily followed today by the modern reader is the amusing *jeu d'esprit, The Art of Political Lying.*

Of his medical writings, his *Essay concerning the Nature of Aliments* (1731) pioneers the literature of dietetics, so popular at the present time, and his *Essay concerning the Effect of Air on the Human Body* showed how advanced he was for his times in scientific research.

Literary criticism, stimulated by such French models as Boileau, had become a thing of vital influence in the hands of Dryden. Thomas Rymer, to whom Dryden refers, was a writer of vigour and ability, but with little of Dryden's insight and sane judgment. "Dryden's criticism", as Johnson said, has " the majesty of a queen; Rymer's has the ferocity of a tyrant."

Neither Rymer nor his successor, John Dennis— another critic of the truculent school—showed any real appreciation of the greatness of Shakespeare. He applied the moral standard to literature with a narrow rigour that sounds strange in modern ears.

More agreeable and informing than Dennis's lucu-brations is Colley Cibber's *Apology for the Life of Mr. Colley Cibber, Comedian* (1740); for with all his excessive vanity and sentimentalism, Cibber was a lively writer and no mean critic of the drama.

(iv) Diarists

An important department of English prose in this period is furnished by the diarists and letter-writers. Their influence was considerable, both upon the development of style and the broadening of subject-matter. They gave colloquial ease and familiarity to the manner, actuality to the matter, and helped to prepare the way for the rich blossoming of fiction that took place during the later years of the period.

Of diarists there were many; we may note the political diary of Narcissus Luttrell (*Brief Historical Relation of State Affairs*, 1678–1714); the " Lives " of Roger North—memoirs of himself and his brothers, of little historic importance but naïvely amusing in style; the more historical and less amusing *Diary* of John Evelyn. Then there is the *Diary* of Henry Sidney, a diplomat at The Hague, dealing with some important negotiations of William III, including some letters of considerable interest from Sir William Temple and others.

The *Diary* of the Countess of Warwick (1625–78), only part of which is now extant, exhibits a writer with a well-marked note of reflective piety in her work. Finally, we have the buoyant, lucid, and high-spirited *Memoirs of Lady Fanshawe*; the tranquil, high-toned *Letters* of Rachel, Lady Russell, the widow of the unfortunate Lord Russell; and the pathetic *Memoirs* of Queen Mary II.

Even among these only two are of special literary importance, the Countess of Warwick and Lady Fanshawe.

But the master diarist is Samuel Pepys.

To his contemporaries Samuel Pepys was little more than a Government official—connected with the Navy Office; to us he is the author of the most fascinating *Diary* in the language. Born in London, February 23, 1633, son of John Pepys, tailor, Samuel spent his early childhood in Kingsland and Hackney.

From St. Paul's to Cambridge (1651)—there he was oft "scandalously overserved with drink" among other matters of a more dignified and academic order. After that we know nothing of his doings until his marriage in 1655, to the pretty and penniless fifteen-year-old daughter of an exiled Huguenot. As he had no money of his own at this time, things would have gone ill had it not been for Sir Edward Montagu (afterwards Lord Sandwich), who took the young couple into his own house and looked after them.

A small clerkship to one of the Exchequer Tellers seemed to Pepys quite a notable affair after this. The salary was £50 and the amount seemed princely to Pepys. And from this time forward his financial fortunes, faithfully recorded, rose steadily. The *Diary* was started in 1660, and in the same year he obtained a position on the Navy Board, worth to him about £250 exclusive of extras. He soon showed considerable ability in the discharge of his duties. Axe Yard is exchanged for Seething Lane, and here lived man and wife for the whole time during which the *Diary* was written—that is to say, for nine years.

His ambition was to become the historian of the Navy, but although he held such a task " sorts mightily with my genius ", he published nothing but some dry *Memoirs*.

In the autumn of 1669 his wife died of a fever. Before this sad event in his life his own bad health, chiefly failing eyesight, compelled him to close his unique *Diary*.

After his retirement in 1690 he lived chiefly at Clapham, where he kept up a friendly correspondence with most of the notable men of the day, including his old comrades Evelyn, Sir Isaac Newton, and Sir Christopher Wren.

He died on May 26, 1703, after months of failing health due to kidney disease, and was buried at St. Olave's, Hart Street, in the same vault as his wife and brother.

It is not easy to read Pepys' character aright. On the one hand, we have the panegyric of his worthy, serious-minded friend Evelyn, who speaks of his " great integrity ", and refers to him as " universally beloved, hospitable, generous, learned in many things, skilled in music, a great cherisher of learned men ". Then there is the frank and ingenuous picture, presented by the diarist himself, of a man inquisitive, childish, clear-headed, vain, ambitious, quarrelsome; one who worked faithfully at his post, yet could abandon himself with zest to the pleasure of the moment. In short, a strange mingling of good and indifferent qualities; sometimes contemptible, never entirely odious. The zest for life, or rather for living, is his most remarkable characteristic. There is scarcely anything which does not interest him in the varied life of the time. It is not the main thoroughfares of life but the side-issues and curious byways that enchain him. London is to him as a box of toys, and he is forever examining her assorted treasures with the gleefulness of a child. Out-of-the-way taverns, new fashions in wearing apparel, the mechanism of a watch, the problems of physiology, cake feasts, shipbuilding, a new dish, an old book, a pretty face—one and all never fail to attract him, and one and all he treats with the same childish inquisitiveness and naïve delight.

He reminds the reader sometimes of Hazlitt, sometimes of George Borrow, in the gusto and exuberant garrulity with which he writes. Yet it is not as a work of art but as a human document that his *Diary* must make its appeal.

One can seè by a glance at the portrait of Pepys that we are dealing with a pleasure-loving, contented, good-hearted man with complex interests. He was no mere *bon viveur*. Fond of music always, he could play four instruments and compose songs. If a supper awakens in him the anticipation of a " glut of pleasure ", he records the " great pleasure " with which he listens to the nightingale. All his delights are violent ones : his emotional sensibility knows no repose; it is always tremulous with some pleasure, whether it be the " infinite delight " of Boyle's *Hydrostatics* or the " warming " comfort of mulled wine. He is always respectable, as the average Londoner is respectable, in his vices and his virtues. Late supper-parties and other " alarums and excursions " are duly expiated by rigid church attendances.

It is hard to sum up Pepys more compendiously and happily than in the phrase of Coleridge—" a pollard man without the top . . . but on this account more broadly branching out from the upper trunk ".

" 1666–67.—To the King's House to ' The Mayd's Tragedy ', but vexed all the while with two talking ladies and Sir Charles Sedley; [1] yet pleased to hear the discourse, he being a stranger. And one of the ladies would and did sit with her mask on all through the play, and being exceedingly witty as ever I heard a woman, did talk most pleasantly with him; but was, I believe, a virtuous woman and of quality. . . . He was mighty

[1] A famous wit and man about town.

witty, and she also making sport with him mighty inoffensively, that more pleasant rencontre I never heard. By that means lost the pleasure of the play wholly, to which both now and then Sir Charles Sedley's exceptions against both words and pronouncing were very pretty."

John Evelyn, the lifelong friend of Pepys, was a man of quite another temperament. He was learned, pedantically careful about his work; scrupulously methodical in his arrangements; an excellent type of the best sort of country gentleman; shrewd and capable in public affairs; large-hearted and loyal as a friend; ready, as Bishop Burnet says, " to contribute everything in his power to perfect other men's endeavours ".

Yet despite his learning and his love of the arts, he is a somewhat colourless writer; when compared with Pepys, his prose, though simple and clear, is easily excelled by other notable prose men of the time.

Born in 1620, at Wotton, of an old Surrey family, John Evelyn received his education at Lewes and Oxford; his antecedents had always been strong supporters of the King and Constitution, so on leaving the University, in 1642, he joined the King's party at Edgehill as a volunteer and later in the year he crossed over to Holland, where he stayed for three months.

When the Civil War broke out in England, Evelyn took advantage of the opportunity to travel extensively on the Continent, and his famous *Diary*, which he kept from 1642 up to the year 1706, owes much to this period in the many rich and graphic descriptions of the public and private collections that he visited. In 1653 he settled down at Sayes Court, near Deptford, and took such an intense interest in his gardens that they were brought almost to the point of perfection; he wrote *Sylva*, a treatise on arboriculture, in 1664, and *Sculptura*, two years earlier, on architecture and the prevention of smoke in London. When the Royal Society took definite form in 1660 he was one of its first members and for some time acted as secretary.

From 1685 to 1687 Evelyn was Commissioner for Privy Seal, and Treasurer of Greenwich Hospital from 1695 to 1703.

After spending forty-two years among the sylvan beauties of Sayes Court, he returned to his birthplace at Wotton, where he died in 1706.

We must not regard Evelyn and Pepys as Restoration editions of the young gentlemen in *Sandford and Merton*. Evelyn was by no means a prig nor, what is equally repellent, a dull dog. Pepys bears testimony to that. Without Pepys' tribute, we might perhaps have had our fears about the social charms of Mr. Evelyn. But when Pepys records the mirthfulness of Evelyn at a party at Greenwich, and how much he contributed to the brightness of the company, we feel reassured.

Chapter Four

The Drama—Davenant to Sheridan

In September 1642 Puritan sentiment, that opposed the drama from the time of Roger Ascham and Philip Stubbes, at last triumphed. The triumph lay rather in the lower vitality of the drama than in the strength of the opponents; for during early Caroline times less and less had it come to voice the spirit of the nation, more and more had it become an entertainment to pander to the dissolute few. Puritanism, now in the political ascendant, put forth its power to crush the obnoxious theatre and the Ordinance of September 2, 1642, commanded the closing of the theatres and the complete suppression of stage plays. Some attempt was made to defy this mandate and met with the prompt reprisal of imprisonment for the actors concerned. Now and again, indeed, during the Commonwealth, a blind eye was turned to private performances "in noblemen's houses", or amid the multifarious festivities of a fair; but the actor's business became too perilous for all save a few intrepid, adventurous souls.

With the exception, therefore, of farcical entertainments of the most popular and boisterous character, known as " droll humour ", and the performance of semi-dramatic pieces with a strong didactic motive to appease the sentiment of the hour during the later years of the Commonwealth, when the embargo was somewhat relaxed, there is nothing in the shape of drama until the Restoration.

Sir William Davenant and James Shirley, survivals from the palmy days of the theatre, saw to the wants of the Court in the early days of its Renascence. Even in their work we can trace clearly the vicissitudes the theatre had suffered. Bound up as it had been with the vicissitudes of Royalty, and suffering, like Royalty, from Puritan anathemas, it had become a Court function and was violently anti-Puritan in feeling.

The influence of France, dominant in the literary ideals of the new age, is clearly discernible in the drama. Comedy became the fashion, and although there are tragedies in this era, they are different in calibre from the Elizabethan tragedy, and far inferior in literary and dramatic value.

Passing from general consideration to the consideration of individual names, that of Dryden is the first to note. His early attempts at play-writing were made in his thirtieth year; although he never achieved any first-rate work in this direction, his productivity was extraordinarily fertile, about thirty plays being placed to his credit. These plays were written, of course, at a time when the first object of the dramatist was to please the King and to cater for those French tastes which had now become prominent.

Starting in *The Wild Gallant* (1663) with a comedy of humour, Jonsonian in pattern, he essayed higher flights in *The Maiden Queen* (1667), *Marriage à la Mode* (1672), and *Amphitryon* (1691). His comedy scenes are better than his tragic efforts, but his wit was not deft enough, nor his humour sufficiently based on first-hand observation of character, to succeed in the theatre.

More successful was his contemporary, " gentle " George Etherege, the companion of Buckhurst. Three plays of merit bear his signature; of these the first, *The Comical Revenge, or Love in a Tub* (1664), is the least interesting, but it has the merit of being amusing without descending to those obscenities too rife in the drama of the time. The second, *She Would if She Could* (1668), is a bright and ingenious play of manners; and the third, *Sir Fopling Flutter* (1676)— decidedly the best—written on similar lines, has something of that dexterous wit carried to so super-lative an excellence by Congreve.

Thomas Shadwell (1642–92), a man of good family and an out-and-out Whig, succeeded Dryden in the Laureateship. He wrote nearly twenty plays and, unlike Etherege, was the reverse of squeamish in his treatment. His merits as a dramatist lie less in his wit, which is never better than Etherege's, often inferior, than in his local colour. With small gift of characterisation, with clumsy technique, he is sur-prisingly alive in his *mise-en-scène*.

His *Squire of Alsatia* (1688), *Epsom Wells* (1676), and *Bury Fair* (1686), are vigorously vital pictures of well-known seventeenth century localities. He is at once one of the worst and one of the best of contemporary writers for the stage.

William Wycherley, born in 1640, came of good Shropshire stock, and his residence in France as a young man stood him in good stead when he began to write.

His first play, *Love in a Wood* (1671), attracted the attention of the Duchess of Cleveland.

In his old age he made the acquaintance of Pope, and died in December 1715.

Love in a Wood and *The Gentleman Dancing-master* (1673) are scarcely above the average by many undistinguished writers of the time; but *The Country Wife* (1675) and *The Plain Dealer* (1677), obviously inspired by Molière's *La Misanthrope*, are, with all their coarseness and occasional prolixities, extremely witty, while the latter play, Wycherley's finest achievement, has the satirical power of Jonson at his best. With much of Shadwell's pictorical skill, he is infinitely superior to him, Etherege, or Dryden, in the bright and vivacious quality of his dialogue.

William Congreve, born 1670, came of good Staffordshire family and was educated at Trinity College, Dublin. His first play, *The Old Bachelor*, had the good fortune to be highly praised by Dryden, and was acted in 1693. *Love for Love* followed in 1695; and *The Way of the World* ushered in the new century. The last, perhaps the most highly esteemed of his plays today, was unsuccessful at the time and, smarting with disappointment, Congreve abruptly gave up his dramatic writing, if we except an occasional masque produced during the last few months of his life.   He died in 1729.

Of his plays, *The Double Dealer*, *Love for Love*, and *The Way of the World* are masterpieces within the limits of the brilliant artificial comedy of the time.   Skilful and apt in intrigue, lively and arresting in characterisation, brilliant in verbal felicities, they revealed at once the weakness and strength of their school.

In *The Way of the World* there are touches, moreover, of emotional power; and *The Mourning Bride* reveals, amid much fustian, some measure of tragic force. But Congreve is, of course, above all things a master of comedy.

In construction and grasp of character, Congreve steadily improved with each succeeding play.   But from the very first he exhibited himself as a master of light and witty dialogue.   He has the easy gaiety of Etherege and the satirical force of Wycherley, and speedily he showed how well he could excel these dramatists in their own lines.

The construction of *The Double Dealer* is greatly superior to *The Old Bachelor*, and the dialogue is rich in happy conceits, but the characterisation is of small account.   It is merely a peg for the author's wit.

Love for Love is on a higher plane.   Here, within well-defined limits, many of the characters have vitality and distinctiveness. There is a farcical strain in the story less happy in invention, but the play as a whole deserves much of the tremendous praise poured on it by Dryden.

In *The Way of the World* we have Congreve at his happiest. Construction, characterisation, dialogue are alike brilliant. The story scarcely matters. But such scenes as those where reputation is murdered by gossip, such characters as Mrs. Millamant and Mirabell, such flashes of wit in the talk between Mrs. Marwood and Mrs. Millamant—or, for the matter of that, any scene where Mrs. Millamant is to the fore—reveal the Restoration at its highest point.

George Farquhar was born at Londonderry in 1678. Like Congreve, he went to Trinity College, Dublin, and afterwards tried " the boards " himself, subsequently joining the army. In personality he is the most volatile and inconsequential of the three later dramatists, loving the good things of life, yet meeting misfortune with an excellent front. He died in 1707.

His plays are *Love and a Bottle*, amusing but thin, and two plays in sequence, in the fashion of Cibber and Vanbrugh, where Peg Woffington had a part that suited her admirably as cheeky Sir Harry. *The Inconstant* (1703) and *The Way to Win Him* have admirably devised scenes; while in *The Recruiting Officer* (1706) and *The Beaux' Stratagem* (1707) he reaches his highest point as a dramatist. The last play especially is unflagging in its humour, and there is an open-air atmosphere about his work (as well as an open-bottle one) that gives it a distinctive place in the Restoration drama.

From 1700 a change began to be discernible in stage productions. It was felt, perhaps, that the appeal was too restricted and, with the spread of coffee-houses, the more general interest in political and social problems, and a change in the manners of the Court, it seemed necessary to strike a more human note.

To attract the general public, especially the steadily growing middle class, some modification was required in the nature of the drama. Colley Cibber (1671–1751) actor, playwright, Laureate, and manager of Drury Lane Theatre, to some extent met this demand, though of his sixteen surviving plays (for instance, *The Careless Husband* and *The Non-Juror*) there is little to be said from point of view of wit and insight, lively and agreeable as they are in parts. More interesting work may be found in the budget of Susannah Centlivre (*c.* 1667–1723), more especially *The Busybody* (1709), and *A Bold Stroke for a Wife* (1717).

Steele essayed to sentimentalise the drama, with no enduring success. George Lillo (1693–1739), pursuing the didactic methods of Steele, achieved some popularity with *George Barnwell*, a melodramatic morality. Henry Fielding, before he found his *métier* in the novel, burlesqued tragedy amusingly in *Tom Thumb*.

George Colman (1732–94), manager of Covent

Garden Theatre, wrote one play at least which has been acted in the present generation—*The Clandestine Marriage*. Farce and comic opera flourished, and some of the best illustrations of this work survive in Mrs. Cowley's (1743–1809) *The Belle's Stratagem*; Macklin's *Man of the World* (1784); Samuel Foote's *Minor* (1760); Townley's *High Life Below Stairs* (1759); Gay's *Beggar's Opera* (1727); while the sentimental drama persisted in Cumberland's *West Indian* (1771), and Holcroft's *Road to Ruin* (1792).

Then towards the end of the century two great names again stand out in relation to the drama, those of Oliver Goldsmith and Richard Brinsley Sheridan.

Goldsmith's *Good-natured Man* (1768) is excellent in parts; *She Stoops to Conquer* (1773) is excellent throughout, with a bright, whimsical humour and fresh charm of dialogue not attained since the days of Congreve. Less witty than the great Restoration dramatists, Goldsmith is greatly superior in his humanity and taste.

A man of profound sympathy with human nature, he aimed as a dramatist at exposing the artificial emotionalism of some contemporaries. And it was on the foundation of human nature, as it is and as he saw it, that he built the success of *She Stoops to Conquer*. Whatever errors critics may find in the play, its characterisation is sound, being both original and recognisably true to life. In structure the play has one central story, easily followed and full of dramatic opportunity. In every scene the geniality of the author is apparent, warming the audience or the reader into friendliness towards him as well as to his stage creatures.

Richard Brinsley Sheridan, born in Dublin, 1751, was the grandson of a witty and brilliant cleric, Dr. Sheridan, the friend of Swift. In 1773 young Sheridan eloped from Bath with the beautiful, accomplished, and short-lived Elizabeth Linley; and his *Rivals*, produced when he was under six-and-twenty, scored an immediate success. Entering Parliament in 1780, he made a reputation on the Whig side as a brilliant speaker, and his speeches against Warren Hastings attracted special attention. He married a second time in 1795, dying in 1816, with bailiffs in the house.

In the first two of his great plays—*The Rivals* and *The School for Scandal*—he combines the comedy of manners with a sentimental admixture only partially successful. Constructively, both plays are remarkably skilful pieces of work, and of their wit it need only be said that they may challenge equality with Congreve and Vanbrugh, with little of their coarseness.

The Critic is written on more broadly farcical lines, but within its limitations it is a rarely delightful piece of extravaganza, displaying a gift of burlesque of the highest order.

With Sheridan, the great age of artificial comedy closes.

In closing this sketch of the drama of the era of Dryden and Pope, we may look at the tragic writings of this time. These, though far inferior both in literary and dramatic importance, are by no means negligible.

Dryden, for instance, proved more happily suited in his " heroic " moods than in his comedy exploits, and *The Maiden Queen* (1667), *Tyrannic Love* (1669), and *The Conquest of Granada* (1670) contain fine passages of rhetoric and impressive scenes. In 1675 appeared his finest play, *Aurengzebe*, in which he turned from the constant use of rhyme and the couplet.

Passing by John Crowne, called "jolly" by Rochester but actually unusually dull, together with Thomas Shadwell and Elkanah Settle, we come to Thomas Otway (1652–85). Otway was undoubtedly next to Dryden in importance. His earlier plays are unimportant, and several versions of French plays follow them. Not until 1680 did he produce a play worthy of his gifts, in *The Orphan*. Two years later came his greatest achievement, *Venice Preserv'd, or a Plot Discover'd.*

The merit of Otway is most difficult to discover; the fact remains that the two plays mentioned have always gripped their audiences. His poetry is often unmusical, marred by colloquialisms, and almost always devoid of verbal beauty. In spite of these defects even his severest critics are pleased to describe *Venice Preserv'd* as the greatest tragedy apart from those of Shakespeare. The reason for his high position seems to lie in the construction of his work and in its manner. He reads badly, but acts well. His construction is sound; the blend of action and

character is good; there is unity and logic in the
events which occur. As far as manner is concerned,
the tragedies are definitely grand, requiring actors of
the " heroic " style, whose gesture and declamation
find the fullest scope in Otway. Given the right production (one not favoured by the theatrical public in
this century), Otway will hold audiences again as well
as he did from his own day until far into the nine-
teenth century.

He died, it is related, through choking during a
meal after a period of poverty and starvation.

Incomparably better than Otway in poetic expression is unfortunate " Nat " Lee (1653?–92). Collaborator of Dryden in various works—e.g. *The Duke
of Guise*—his own tragedies are weak in plot and
situation. Even his poetry is unequal, partly
because insanity deprived him of the quietness of
mind necessary to critical revision of his lines. His
The Rival Queens (1677) was an immediate success;
he followed it by *Mithridates, King of Pontus* (1678)
and by another eminently successful tragedy, *Theo-
dosius, or the Force of Love* (1680).

Lee wrote chiefly in a pseudo-heroic Blank Verse,
mixed with passages in an equally pseudo-Heroic
Couplet and periods of prose. His verse forms are
far less important than his ability to use the right word,
and to use it inspiredly as had Marlowe and Shakespeare. This is the source of the movement and colour
in his lines. Like Otway's, they require declamatory
style for full effectiveness.

Nicholas Rowe (1674–1718) deserves credit for work not directly connected with the writing of drama, although he earned his place as an author. As Shakespeare's first biographer, he deserves notice. As his first editor, he merits the greatest approbation, for, inaccurate as some of his work necessarily was, he painstakingly divided his Fourth-Folio text into Acts and Scenes, inserted clear stage directions, and made many emendations in the text which later editors were glad to incorporate without acknowledgment. Rowe was appointed Poet Laureate at the accession of George I.

As a dramatist he is known by *The Fair Penitent* (1703) (not original in plot, but giving the proto-type on which Richardson modelled his Lovelace in *Clarissa Harlowe*) and notably by *Jane Shore* (1714), in which he imitated Shakespeare and provided Mrs. Siddons with a favourite part. Indeed, Rowe's female characters are usually more effective than his villains and gallants.

The most important dramatist of the time is Thomas Southerne (1660–1746), but his importance is not literary. His first remarkable play was *The Fatal Marriage* (1694), with an equally fatal sub-title (*or the Innocent Adultery*), which gave the theatrical world an opening for jokes which lasted longer than the play. Rather better was *Oroonoko, or the Royal Slave* (1696). The tragedies are a mixture of Blank Verse and prose, contain unmistakable tragic power but are nearer to sensation than real drama.

The decadence of the tragic drama which these notes show may be attributed to the convention of the age in which the tragedies appeared. Poetry itself was artificial. Emotionalism was not desired; verse was preferred smooth and pleasing in metrical evenness. Thus the habit of the time was against any progress in tragic drama.

Moreover, the public did not wish to see tragedy. The reaction against the Puritan ideals of the Commonwealth inclined people to more frivolous entertainment and, in the theatre, to comedy. Consequently dramatists had little heart for tragedy—a fact which may be observed in the number of plays which were merely revisions of plots found in the works of Shakespeare and his contemporaries. Even Dryden tried to base a play (*All for Love*) on *Antony and Cleopatra*.

At this time, too, opera made its appearance as a rival to drama. As might be expected, Dryden produced remarkable examples of this derivative of the Masque (e.g. *Albion and Albanius* in 1685). But this form of play, as heroic as the tragedy, encountered the serious drama's other rivals, the tendency towards comedy and away from serious sentiment in verse. It changed its course and Gay wrote *The Beggar's Opera*, the perfect expression of the taste of the theatre audience.

Chapter Five

Another View of the Age

IF certain aspects of social life in the eighteenth century are reflected in the writings of Addison, Steele, and Pope, we must consider men like Johnson, Fielding, and Hogarth if we would learn something of the sterner matter of the times. For there was another world outside the leisurely and urbane visitation of the *Spectator*—a dark underworld of want and misery, of fierce primal passion and desperate resolve. Fielding and Smollett had tarried there for a while; the tragic figure of Richard Savage never emerges from the gloom; one recalls the gaunt wretchedness of scribblers like Boyes and Derrick, whom Johnson befriended, the hack work to which Defoe's genius had perforce to stoop in order that he might live, and those political journalists about whom *Pendennis* has much to say. Finally, there is that quaint, delightful, impecunious Irishman, Oliver Goldsmith. But the great, uncouth, burly, lovable figure of Johnson will serve our purpose. No one knew the underworld better than Johnson, or sympathised more practically with its dwellers.

The London of Johnson was a noisy, turbulent, high-spirited London. But the old gaiety, the picturesque festivals of the City before Puritanism had frowned over its pleasures, were no longer to be seen. Maypoles had disappeared and with them the genuine music and poetry of the open-air had also gone. Domesticity and the tavern conspired together to give a blow to the old social life of the streets.

Violence, indeed, is the key-note of the social life. It permeates every grade of society, and people become rougher and grimmer as we descend in the social scale.

Grub Street had existed before Johnson's time; there was a Grub Street in the time of Robert Greene, sinner and moralist, and of happy-go-lucky Nash; ever since the age of Marlowe the literary vagabonds of the day had gathered at the tavern, and the author of *The Jew of Malta* was not the only one to perish in a drunken brawl. During the Civil Wars, when the pamphleteer sprang into being, Grub Street numbered its devotees. Want and necessity, those hungry wolves, claimed among their victims the sweet singer Edmund Waller and the brilliant Otway.

However, it must be admitted that the lot of the writer was improving during the century. When one remembers the few pounds that came from *Paradise Lost*, seven hundred pounds for *Tom Jones* seems quite an impressive sum.

The impecuniosity of men of letters was not due entirely to public indifference : extravagance and improvidence played their share in the tale of mean streets. Samuel Boyes, whose clothes had been got out of pawn owing to the generous exertions of Johnson, would spend his last few shillings to buy truffles and mushrooms to add relish to his bit of meat; then, when all his money was spent, he would take to his bed, cover himself with a blanket and, through holes made in this covering, he would cheerfully continue to write.

One of the most remarkable of Johnson's early companions was Richard Savage, poet and vagabond. Johnson describes him as " of middle stature, of a thin habit of body, of long visage, coarse features, and melancholy aspect ". He made his acquaintance in 1737, and they would often roam the streets together; on one occasion they walked up and down St. James's Square for several hours, denouncing Sir Robert Walpole and making resolutions to " stand by their country ".

Savage, far inferior to Johnson both in character and intellect, had acquired, through travelling about the world, a comprehensive knowledge of men and things, which naturally impressed the young, responsive Johnson.

It is typical of Johnson that he should try so desperately hard to paint an attractive picture of his old companion ; the best thing to be recorded of Savage is his friendship for Johnson. Many men had befriended Savage, including Steele, but he ill repaid his friends ; and few could have lamented when he died at last in a debtor's prison.

Garrick did much to raise the tone of the drama, and a noticeable feature of the age was the increasing interest in the theatre among the middle classes. The Shakespearean revivals brought forward a number of notable actresses. Then, as now, the young and exquisite and ladies of fashion went as much to be seen as to see.

Garrick endeavoured to clear the stage of all except the actors. He also much improved the lighting effects by introducing footlights in place of the circular chandelier hitherto suspended over the stage.

A notable addition to the serious recreation of Londoners was the British Museum. The British Museum was once situated in a " noble suburb ". Bloomsbury had at this time very fine houses and large gardens, flanked by country lanes and pretty cottages.

The library and collection which Sir Hans Sloane, the well-known doctor, had got together was offered to the country for a nominal £20,000. The Treasury at the time did not care to advance the money, and the House of Commons chose to order the issue of a State Lottery (26 Geo. II, c. 22) ; 100,000 tickets at £3 each were issued, £200,000 being spent in prizes, varying from £10,000 to £10. The remaining £100,000 was placed to the credit of the British Museum Purchase Fund. Not only was the Sloane Collection bought but the Harleian and Cottonian manuscripts were acquired. Moreover, Montague House was purchased, so that the Museum was thrown open to the public in 1759.

For the less seriously inclined there was the sorry sport of cock-fighting, which was as popular in

Johnson's day as in FitzStephen's. It occupied the same place in popular estimation as horse-racing does to-day.

There was a decided change for the worse in the manners of the early eighteenth century; the polish of the Restoration period had worn off and now manners and morals were fairly well balanced. The early Georges, with their boorish tastes, set no grand standard of courtesy and refinement; and Ministers like Walpole harmonised uncommonly well with the general atmosphere of the Court.

Masquerades—an extremely popular and roisterous relaxation—were first held at the King's Theatre in the Haymarket, and the " quality " assembled in Ranelagh Gardens, Chelsea, or in Vauxhall, for " the garden is pleasanter and one goes by water ".

We have seen something of the estimates of woman-kind by men like Addison and Pope. In the earlier years of the century woman was regarded, when not as a plaything, at any rate as little better than a house-keeper. But about the year 1760 a change took place in the status of women.

Mrs. Montague, a friend of the Duchess of Port-land, attempted a reform of manners by inaugurating parties " where cards could not be thought of ", but " where the fair sex might participate in conversation with literary and ingenious men ".

Other ladies had their special groups, and in this way the literary women of the day met and fraternised together—Hannah More, Mrs. Thrale, Hannah Cowley (author of *The Belle's Stratagem*), and Frances Burney.

In approaching the close of the eighteenth century, observant of occasional signs that its literary modes must change, we are faced by the problem of where to draw the line between the Augustan and the Romantic writers. Side by side with the dominance of the Conventional we have Cowper already opening windows to Nature as she is in the woods and fields. Here also is Blake—one of the most important poets of the time, but quite out of step with its by now traditional principles and outlook. How are we to apportion this history, so that it can present a reasonably clear account of the agents at work in the progress of literature, without the narrative undergoing too much complication?

Perhaps the question answers itself. We are still under the influence of the great four of the century, Dryden, Pope, Addison, Johnson. Let us go on with them to the end, so far as chronology allows by a proper latitude. Thus we shall deal with Cowper, but not with Blake. We will see the Augustan age through before scrutinising it closely for signs of the age which is to follow.

By doing this we will be better able to detail the causes which maintained the Augustan ideals almost to the last year of the century.

The first of these is probably the influence of Dr. Johnson. Although his mind was always hungry for knowledge and vigorous in the examination of ideas, the " Great Cham " was conservative where self-expression was involved. This attitude is attributable, especially in the matter of poetry, to his belief and to his sensibility. For he believed, as he wrote in *Rasselas*, that the business of the poet " is to examine not the individual but the species; to remark general properties and large appearances. He does not number the streaks of the tulip. . . ." And Mrs. Piozzi testifies to his sensitiveness, in writing " Of the pathetic in poetry he never liked to speak ". The reason she gives is remarkable : " He was more strongly and more violently affected by the force of words representing ideas capable of affecting him at all than any other man in the world, I believed."

Now, Johnson's influence on the reading public as well as on the writers of his day was greater than we may easily comprehend. To all except the few who were impelled by individuality of taste he was an almost infallible mentor—a fact seriously if humorously acknowledged by Thackeray in *Vanity Fair* and by Mrs. Gaskell in *Cranford*. The Romantics came to hate the posthumous influence of the man who had been the sage, the philosopher, the supreme arbiter of English letters. The Augustan tradition, beside which the writings of Blake, Cowper, and Collins were of negligible effect, was supported by the massive solidity of Johnson's reputation. The prose of Addison, the verse of Dryden and Pope, the perfection each form had acquired for the purposes deemed suitable to literature, were all supported by Johnson, who would well have agreed with Pope's dictum that manner was more important than matter—" what oft was thought but ne'er so well expressed " being a principle of eighteenth-century criticism.

A further cause of the lingering of the Augustan age through the late years of the century was ignorance of the ages which had preceded it. Gray alone had any real knowledge of medievalism; the learning of Temple or Collins smelt too much of the lamp to become widely effective; MacPherson's Ossianic forgeries, like Chatterton's Rowley poems, created sensation, and thereby lost their chance to be taken seriously as having value in themselves. Percy's *Reliques of Ancient English Poetry* affected the trend of literary development, but the book did not appear until 1765, and was intended to attract attention to former days rather than to compel it. The work of Thomas Warton and his sons brought forward Chaucer and revived some interest in Spenser and Milton. More important, perhaps, they helped to break the long interval, between Milton and Wordsworth, in which the sonnet languished.

In 1802 Wordsworth could write :

> Scorn not the Sonnet; Critic, you have frowned,
> Mindless of its just honours; with this key
> Shakespeare unlock'd his heart . . .

Yet for 100 years, except for the work of the Wartons and of William Lisle Bowles, the sonnet had scarcely existed in English literature.

Additional to these two reactionary influences, we

must reckon the habit of mind found in those who pride themselves on their civilised manners. The eighteenth century was essentially a time of manners and of " civil ways ". In the end the form is mistaken for the spirit it was shaped to house. Empires as well as literatures have succumbed to the hardening effects of established modes. We find it difficult in our days, when everything is fluid and uncertain, to realise how set was the eighteenth-century mind against change. A prose of excellence had been built up; the vagaries of poetic form and imagination had been controlled by the establishment of settled numbers and clearly defined lines. All was well. Let what had been continue to be accepted. New things were stirring, new movements and thoughts making an occasional appearance, new experiments presenting their ugliness for approval. Here were

Beauty that shocks you, parts that none can trust.

As the century draws to its close, with lyrics, and prose disturbingly undignified, and a new way of looking at real fields and real flowers (so often more disappointing than those found in the images of Dyer or Thomson), the majority of readers said what we also might have said : " Let the Peace of the Augustans continue, with its charm, its measured delights, its soothing smoothness, its elegance, and its graciousness." We might have said that because even we turn again and again to its sweet beauty, its abstract loveliness. . . .

Silent Nymph, with curious eye !
Who, in the purple evening, lie
On the mountain's lonely van,
Beyond the noise of busy man,
Painting fair the forms of things.
While the yellow linnet sings.

Even the romantic might wish to repose longer in
the timeless, undisturbed possession of that peace.

And see the rivers how they run,
Thro' woods and meads, in shade and sun,
Sometimes swift, sometimes slow,
Wave succeeding wave, they go,
A various journey to the deep,
Like human life to endless sleep !

Chapter Six

Poetry—Thomson to Cowper

(i) Secular Poets

THE eighteenth century is an age of great prose and, until its close, of second-rate poetry. In the closing years a change took place in the character of its verse, which gradually became more and more pronounced, and finally led to the splendid outburst of Romantic poetry in the dawn of the new century.

The change is manifest so far back as Thomson's *Winter* in 1726 and, although many verse-writers of the time elected to follow the school of Pope, and continued to eschew passion and naturalism in verse, from Thomson onwards there is a steady output of verse that reflects a more intimate relation with Nature.

James Thomson was born in 1700, at Ednam in Roxburghshire. In 1725 he came to London and became tutor in Lord Binning's family. His poem cycle, *The Seasons*, begun in 1726, was finished in 1730 with *Autumn*. These poems met with considerable esteem and, despite his indifferent success in other directions, he made a sufficient number of influential friends to find security for the rest of his days. He was a kindly and agreeable man, with poor initiative, so it is fortunate for him that he was looked after in the

way of appointments and pensions. He died in
1748.

As a writer he signalised the departure from the
town to the country, chose the Spenserian stanza and
Blank Verse as his medium, and eschewed the stopped
couplet that was ubiquitous in the realm of poetry at
the time. He was a copious producer, but his best
work lies in *Winter, Spring, Summer*, and *Autumn*
(*The Seasons*), and in *The Castle of Indolence*. His long
poem on "Liberty" is flat and uninspiring, and his
plays, though fairly successful, are insignificant from
the literary point of view. In his masque *Alfred*,
written in conjunction with David Mallett, the lyric
of "Rule Britannia" occurs, afterwards republished
with Thomson's initials; its vigorous swashbuckling
scarcely suggests the fat and indolent poet.

There is greater ease, and more plastic imagination,
in *The Castle of Indolence* (1748), a fantastic poem that
reproduces happily an atmosphere of dreamy melancholy, enlivened now and again by mirthful passages.

The Castle of Indolence

Joined in the prattle of the purling rills
Were heard the lowing herds along the vale,
And flocks loud bleating from the distant hills,
And vacant shepherds piping in the dale :
And, now and then, sweet Philomel would wail,
Or stock-doves plain amid the forest deep,
That drowsy rustled to the sighing gale;
And still a coil the grasshopper did keep,
Yet all these sounds blent, inclined all to sleep.

Full in the passage of the vale, above,
A sable, silent, solemn forest stood;
Where nought but shadowy forms was seen to move,
As Idlesse fancied in her dreaming mood;
And up the hills, on either side, a wood
    Of Blackening pines, ay waving to and fro,
Sent forth a sleepy horror through the blood;
And where this valley winded out, below,
The murmuring main was heard, and scarcely heard, to flow.

A pleasing land of drowsy-hed it was,
Of dreams that wane before the half-shut eye;
And of gay castles in the clouds that pass,
Forever flushing round a summer-sky:
There eke the soft delights, that witchingly
Instil a wanton sweetness through the breast,
And the calm pleasures always hovered nigh;
But whate'er smacked of noyance, or unrest,
Was far, far off expelled from this delicious nest.

Among Thomson's disciples may be mentioned
John Armstrong (1709–79), also a Roxburghshire
man, and the political versifier, Richard Glover (1712–
85).

Armstrong was a physician, and made strenuous
attempts to treat dietetics and hygiene from the poet's
standpoint, in his *Art of Preserving Health* (1744).   He
was certainly never blessed with a sense of humour
or he would not have spoken of a cold bath as " a
gelid cistern ".   In his favour it may be said that his
Blank Verse is agreeable and sometimes impressive,
and even his medical stanzas—like those added to *The
Castle of Indolence*—have some felicities of diction.

If Armstrong is prolix Glover's fatal fluency is

overwhelming. It would be interesting to know how many readers have waded through the thirty books of *The Athenaid* (1787), or even the comparative trifle, *Leonidas* (1737) in nine books.

His best claim to remembrance lies in his breezy and effective ballad, *Admiral Hosier's Ghost*.

John Dyer, painter and cleric (1700 ?–58), is remembered for his *Grongar Hill* and *Country Walk*, poems faulty in technique but fresh and observant in character.

Robert Blair (1699–1746), with *The Grave*, is akin to Young in his portentous gravity; and Matthew Green (1698–1733), a Custom-House clerk, follows in the wake of Swift, though *The Spleen* is certainly more genial in its satire than the verse of the sardonic creator of Gulliver.

William Shenstone (1714–63) calls for more detailed notice. Perhaps his first claim to gratitude is his share in preparing Percy's *Reliques*, in which collection he would have been co-editor had not death ended his labour. In himself Shenstone was a mixture of desire for poetic fame and fear of missing it. " I wanted to write *one* good song and could never please myself," he said. His experiments include odes, songs, elegies, ballads, in octosyllabic couplets, Heroic Couplets, and Blank Verse. His most celebrated piece is *The School-mistress*, written as a kindly parody of the Spenserian manner. It catches the true pastoral note of his own age, as also do the four parts of the excellent *A Pastoral Ballad*, in which he successfully uses an anapæstic trimeter pattern. Of his short pieces the best known to-day is *Written at an Inn at Henley*, from *The Levities*. Its conclusion may be given as a reminder :

> And now once more I shape my way
> Thro' rain or shine, thro' thick or thin,
> Secure to meet, at close of day,
> With kind reception at an inn.
>
> Who'er has travell'd life's dull round,
> Where'er his stages may have been,
> May sigh to think he still has found
> The warmest welcome, at an inn.

An agreeable prose writer with some critical faculty, and a dexterous and fluent maker of verse, he deserves notice as being characteristic of the transition period, breaking away in certain directions from the eighteenth century conventions. Yet he had insufficient force to strike out a really original line. Sometimes he reminds us of the sentimental side of Goldsmith.

Passing to William Collins (1721–59), we find another step in the transitional movement has been gained. Here, as in the case of Thomson, we have to note the combination of an often artificial and pedantic style with a delicate and intimate poetic vision.

Early afflicted by mental derangement, and by poverty, from which publishers rescued him by literary commissions, Collins inevitably produced poetry at irregular intervals and of uneven quality. A legacy brought him financial security but shortly afterwards his insanity became chronic. Consequently his total output was small. Among his best-known pieces are the *Ode to Evening*, one of the some dozen poems in this form, *The Passions, an Ode for Music*; the exquisite *Dirge in Cymbeline*; *How Sleep the Brave* being one of his most popular poems.

There is in Collins a genuine lyric note which is true and exquisite. At the same time (and his mental illness may have been partly responsible for the fact) he strikes us as often wanting true emotion. That is to say, our impression is that he has been to some pains to secure the feeling which he thought he ought to have. The result is a degree of coolness, a kind of premeditation, which some readers consider a defect in his work. For others it is one of his more attractive qualities ! Wherever the truth may lie between these extremes, to say that Collins sought inspiration rather than possessed it is not to say he was a poor poet. Writers greater than he have defined the limits of their poetic material and have been better poets for so doing.

Indeed, if we pay due attention to the inspiration in Collins, we find more of it than we may have expected. The poet Gray, with whom he is invariably but not too reasonably compared, has more artifice in weaving a wealth of classical allusion almost imperceptibly into his verses and a perfect technique for working his lines into elaborate beauties of music and colour. For these reasons an easy judgment may be made that he is the better poet. More careful consideration, however, may lead to some uncertainty as to whether there is not more real poetry in the *Ode to Evening* than in any poem by Gray. In the comparative simplicity of Collins is found one of his greatest merits, although it has not always been admitted to be such when comparison with Gray is made.

To compare the two poets is a mistake. They must be judged separately, or we shall be reduced to quoting :

> Now fades the glimmering landscape on the sight,
>   And all the air a solemn stillness holds,
> Save where the beetle wheels his droning flight,
>   And drowsy tinklings lull the distant folds . . .

on behalf of Gray and, on behalf of Collins :

> Now air is hush'd, save where the weak-eyed bat
> With short shrill shriek flits by on leathern wing,
>   Or where the beetle winds
>   His small but sullen horn . . .

A debate of this kind must necessarily be inconclusive, since it is ultimately found to be about nothing essential to the poetic value of either poet.

It is better to assess Gray for his own qualities, and to evaluate Collins because he gave us stanzas such as these :

> For when thy folding-star arising shows
> His paly circlet, at his warning lamp
>   The fragrant hours, and elves
>   Who slept in buds the day,

> And many a nymph who wreathes her brows with sedge,
>   And sheds the freshening dew, and, lovelier still,
>   The pensive pleasures sweet,
>   Prepare thy shadowy car :

Then lead, calm votaress, where some sheety lake
Cheers the lone heath, or some time-hallow'd pile,
    Or upland fallows grey
    Reflect its last cool gleam.

Incidentally, we may note in this brief extract how
Collins, for all his precision of classical form, stood
apart from the Augustan tradition.   For the lines are
actually not as classical as they appear (their metre is
broken into lengths quite novel to that age), and Nature
although decorously habited in eighteenth-century
fashion, is true Nature, and not a conventional
abstraction.

It is surprising to know that Thomas Gray (1716–
71) of *Elegy in a Country Churchyard* fame was regarded
by his contemporaries as a revolutionary rather obscure
in meaning but shocking none the less.   When *The
Bard* and *The Progress of Poesy* appeared in 1757, their
" wildness " was considered alarming.   Perhaps the
poems were the more alarming because they came
from a man known to be a scholar of modestly affluent
circumstances, who lived at Cambridge and had
recently refused the Laureateship.

A man of independent mind, with a genius for
friendship (his *Letters* are among the most delightful
in our literature), he was wholly indifferent to public
opinion.   Immersed in his studies of old English and
Welsh and Norse, he allowed his poems to circulate
in manuscript, so that most of them were unpublished
at the time of his death.   They were then edited by
his poet friend, William Mason, who freely altered

them to read as he thought Gray should have amended them. However, modern texts are reasonably satisfactory restorations of the original writing.

His most famous poems are *Ode on the Spring*, *Ode on a Distant Prospect of Eton College*, *Hymn to Adversity*, *Ode on the Pleasure arising from Vicissitude*, apart from the two previously mentioned and the *Elegy*. Opinion about them has varied. Matthew Arnold awarded Gray a position among the greatest, even though he had refused " to speak out " in his verses; Professor Saintsbury demurred, remarking that there was nothing to speak out about.

Whether a study of Gray will lead us to favour one or the other of these opinions, we see in Gray a facility for handling the quatrain stanza without the least trace of monotony—no easy feat to achieve—and a delicacy of phrasing wholly admirable. Behind these virtues there is a curiously personal quality which suffuses the lines with the soft light of something never clear enough for us to define. Is it the glory of true inspiration ? Or is it a skill suggestive of something really not in Gray at all ? Only a discriminating taste can decide the point. The value of Gray is one of the pleasantest literary problems each reader has to encounter. Those who remember his indolence, his complete indifference to reputation, his scholarly retirement, may believe that, writing primarily for himself, Gray was fastidiously pleased only to suggest the power of his perception and emotion.

It is the personal quality of this power or, if it is

preferred, of his skill to insinuate its presence, which makes the poet unique. There can be only one Thomas Gray. And, not to be too withdrawn from positive opinion about him, we may say definitely that his two odes (*Eton College* and *Pleasure arising from Vicissitude*) and the unique *Elegy* (for all that it is mis-named, being in no way really elegiac), are incomparably fine poems in the completely personal manner of Gray.

> Now the golden Morn aloft
>   Waves her dew-bespangled wing,
> With vermeil cheek and whisper soft
>   She woos the tardy Spring :
> Till April starts, and calls around
> The sleeping fragrance from the ground,
> And lightly o'er the living scene
> Scatters his freshest, tenderest green.
>
> New-born flocks, in rustic dance,
>   Frisking play their feeble feet;
> Forgetful of their wintry trance
>   The birds in presence greet;
> But chief, the sky-lark, warbles high
> His trembling, thrilling ecstasy;
> And lessening from the dazzled sight,
> Melts into air and liquid light.

David Malloch (who later changed his name to Mallet) was a pleasant writer of light verse and a faithful disciple alternately of his friend Thomson and of Pope.

Mark Akenside (1721–70), like John Armstrong, was a physician. The son of a butcher, and originally intended for the ministry, he became interested in physics, and his *Pleasures of the Imagination* appeared about the same time as Armstrong's *Art of Preserving Health*.

As a writer, he is neither pronouncedly of the school of Thomson nor of that of Pope, inclining perhaps to that of Dryden.   His abilities are only mediocre, but he has been often under-estimated as a writer and, if his verses lack the polish of Pope and the easy force of Dryden, there are touches in them, in the *Odes* and *The Epistle to Curio* especially, of genuine feeling and sincerity.

(ii) Writers of Devotional Verse

Isaak Watts (1674–1748) has come down to posterity as the author of *Let Dogs Delight* and *The Busy Bee*, and these moral songs for children have survived both Watts's considerable contribution to hymnology and his more considerable but often grotesquely poor contributions to secular poetry.   It is to Watts's credit that he broke away from the monotony of the favourite couplet and proved himself at times an able if unequal metrist.

Too early to feel the reaction against the school of Pope, his work is properly looked upon as transitional and, had he been born later, it is probable he would by temperament and feeling have belonged to the new school of romantic naturalism.

Greater than Watts in imaginative power, and more advantageously placed in point of time, is Charles Wesley (1708–88).   To find his equal as a writer of sacred song one has to turn to the religious poetry of the seventeenth century, and not even in Vaughan and Herbert do we find such intensity of personal feeling and experience as meets us in the verse of Wesley. Moreover, there is more lyrical fire in " Jesus, Lover of my Soul " than in all of Watts's hymns; but from the purely poetical point of view Wesley's highest reach is made in the verses on *Wrestling Jacob*.

Wrestling Jacob

Come, O thou traveller unknown,
    Whom still I hold, but cannot see;
My company before is gone,
    And I am left alone with thee;
With thee all night I mean to stay,
And wrestle till the break of day.

I need not tell thee who I am,
    My misery and sin declare;
Thyself hast called me by my name,
    Look on thy hands and read it there !
But who, I ask thee, who art thou ?
Tell me thy name, and tell me now.

Christopher Smart (1722–71) has been as exaggeratedly praised after a period of neglect as is usual in those circumstances.   Educated at Durham and Cambridge, he secured a Fellowship at Pembroke College. The greater part of his life was broken up by recurring insanity, a fact to be remembered when reading the more extravagant passages in his poetry.   Among a good deal of undistinguished work, he achieved real merit in a few slight pieces written after the manner of Samuel Butler or Swift.

His main value is found in the hundred stanzas of *A Song to David*, composed during a lucid interval. Filled with Biblical imagery, for us curiously reminiscent of Blake, written in the six-lined Romance stanza, the poem has a sweep and rush which hurries it triumphantly over its defects to a rhapsody of sound.

> He sang of God—the mighty source
> Of all things—the stupendous force
>   On which all strength depends;
> From whose right arm, beneath whose eyes,
> All period, power, and enterprise
>   Commences, reigns, and ends.

> Tell them, I Am, Jehovah said
> To Moses; while earth heard in dread,
>   And, smitten to the heart,
> At once above, beneath, around,
> All Nature, without voice or sound,
>   Replied, O Lord, Thou Art.

The poem is by no means all tempest. The following stanzas show something of his not wholly normal quaintness, of his striking turn of thought, and of his delicacy of idea and expression.

> For Adoration, in the dome
> Of Christ, the sparrows find a home
>   And on His olives perch:
> The swallow also dwells with thee,
> O man of God's humility,
>   Within his Saviour's church.

> Sweet is the dew that falls betimes,
> And drops upon the leafy limes,
>   Sweet, Hermon's fragrant air :
> Sweet is the lily's silver bell,
> And sweet the wakeful taper's smell
>   That watch for early prayer.

(iii) Miscellaneous Poets

Returning to secular poetry, nothing need be said of Gray's friend, William Mason, who copied most of Gray's weaknesses, with scarcely a touch of his power, and of William Falconer, who wrote the *Shipwreck*, except that they broke away from the couplet form and from the conventional subject-matter of their times. The brothers Warton, Thomas and Joseph, were more remarkable as critics than as verse-writers, for they showed real appreciation of Elizabethan poetry. Thomas was Laureate from 1785 until his death, and his poetry belongs largely to the school of Pope, though not without suggestions of Gray.

Charles Churchill, born in 1731, at Westminster, took Orders in 1756, but soon realised his unsuitability for the clerical profession. Reckless in spirit, and dissolute in character, he proved himself a vigorous satirist on the actors of the day, in the *Rosciad*, and a vitriolic one as well, as his epistle to William Hogarth testifies :

> Thy body shrivell'd up, thy dim eyes sunk
> Within their sockets deep, thy weak hands shrunk,
> The body's weight unable to sustain,
> The stream of life scarce trembling thro' the vein,

More than half-kill'd with honest truths, which fell,
Thro' thy own fault, from men who wish'd thee well,
Can'st thou, e'en thus, thy thoughts to vengeance give,
And, dead to all things else, to malice live ?
Hence, Dotard, to thy closet ! Shut thee in,
By deep repentance wash away thy sin;
From haunts of men to shame and sorrow fly,
And, on the verge of death, learn to die.

Hogarth, who was, as a matter of fact, dying at this time, took the lampoon acutely to heart.

In Churchill the fires of the school of Dryden and Butler leap up for the last time. His vigour and power are as obvious as his violence and savagery.

James Beattie (1735–1803), born in Kincardineshire and educated at Aberdeen, is another illustration of the mediocre writer whose work, though possessing little intrinsic value, interests us as literary students for its genuine attempt to bring emotion back into poetry, to find inspiration in the romantic past, and to eschew the school of epigrammatic cleverness and artifice. Neither *The Minstrel* nor *The Progress of Genius* can afford us much æsthetic pleasure. But his work is a step farther towards romanticism away from classicism, and shows renewed interest in the Spenserean stanza.

On the same plane are John Langhorne and William Mickle. Langhorne's *Country Justice* deals with rural life in a way that reminds us of Crabbe rather than of any contemporary. He shows unmistakably the trend of the new movement. Mickle's *Songs and Ballads* stimulated the taste for ballad, more strikingly effected in Percy's *Reliques*. Among these re-clothed old songs and modern imitations is the well-known *There is nae Luck aboot the Hoose*. His poem *Cumnor Hall* is a pleasant, sentimental piece which inspired Scott to write *Kenilworth*.

Last relics of the school of Pope, who succeeded in bringing about its downfall even more quickly than the pioneers of romanticism, are Erasmus Darwin (1731–1802) and William Hayley (1745–1820). Darwin was a physician who lived at Lichfield. He was an able scientist, and in his *Zoonomia* (1794) wrote a thoughtful treatise on the laws of organic life. Unhappily he tried to popularise science by writing in verse form and, in *The Botanic Garden* and *The Economy of Vegetation*, he gave the public bombastic and absurd pieces of work, which in place of making science attractive made poetry ridiculous.

Hayley had no more imagination, nor as a poet had he Darwin's genuine value as a scientist. His dull artificiality is equalled only by his dismal fluency. These men are said to have brought about the final downfall of the older school of verse. The future was with the Romantics.

In contrast with them stands Thomas Chatterton. Born at Bristol in 1752, the son of a schoolmaster and cathedral singer, he had a fitful education and was bound to an attorney in 1764. Brought up in the atmosphere of St. Mary Redcliffe, he haunted the building, and soon began to imitate certain medieval documents he found therein. Thus started the series of forgeries known as the *Rowley Poems*. Hinting

that he had discovered valuable old Mss., he soon
found some to believe in the ballads, interludes, and
the like which he gave out as belonging to a certain
Rowley of Bristol.   He attracted the notice of Horace
Walpole and came to London, April 1770.   For a
time he eked out a pittance by his work, but the
demand fell off and, too proud to beg, he poisoned
himself with arsenic in his Holborn lodgings, in August
1770.

He was a skilful metrist, with a clever gift of imitation and touches of real romantic feeling, sometimes
expressed with delicate spontaneity, at others in purely
conventional language.   The unevenness of his work,
however, is a youthful quality which need not be
dwelt upon; the imaginative power displayed in the
Rowley Poems is sufficiently remarkable, and his influence upon the poets of the Romantic revival,
though exaggerated by some critics, was no doubt
considerable.

Before the death of Johnson, two pleasing poets
appeared, who very definitely ushered in the new era—
Cowper and Crabbe. They are best studied as
pioneers rather than representatives of Romanticism,
for in each of them the conventions of the eighteenth
century lingered, and their work, to an extent, still
participated in the character of the transitional period.

(iv) Cowper and Crabbe

There is perhaps no more pathetic life-story in the
history of our literature than that of William Cowper.

His father's death in 1756 threw Cowper on his own resources, and the loss of his home at the parsonage was a real grief to him.

In 1763 a nomination to the post of Clerk of the Journals of the House of Commons was secured; his nominee's right to appoint being disputed, Cowper was summoned to an examination; but magnifying this simple ordeal excessively—" mortal poison " he called it—so unhinged his brain that he attempted self-destruction. After this—suffering from religious melancholia that troubled him more or less throughout his life—he resided for eighteen months with Dr. Cotton, at St. Albans.

On leaving St. Albans he made the acquaintance of the Rev. Morley Unwin, his wife and their son and daughter; and thus, induced to make one of their family party, he gained once more the advantages of home life. The following year, however, Mr. Unwin died, but his death made no difference to Cowper; he merely removed with Mrs. Unwin and her daughter to Olney on the banks of the Ouse, where his friend John Newton was curate, and here he wrote about seventy of the *Olney Hymns*.

In 1773 a second period of darkness clouded his life for three years, but again he recovered and began to make poetry the business of his life.

In 1782 he published a volume of poems, in addition to the delightful ballad, *John Gilpin*, the result of a story told him by the vivacious Lady Austen, also the instigator of his more ambitious work, *The Task*, published in 1785. From this time Cowper takes his place among the finest English poets.

In 1786 his cousin, Lady Hesketh, persuaded him and Mrs. Unwin to remove to Weston. They did so. Cowper was now in easy circumstances by the grant of a pension of £300, and began translating at the rate of " forty lines a day " the *Homer* he published in 1791. Notwithstanding the relief and distractions found in many directions—his taming three young hares is well known—and the kindness of his friends, another awful night-time darkened his life, and from this time, 1794, up to the time of his death on April 25, 1800, very few glimpses of light were vouchsafed him, the poem *On the Receipt of my Mother's Picture* being written in a lucid interval.

In the technique of his work, Cowper belongs to the old rather than to the new. He shows neither power nor the wish to break away from the old metrical forms. Some of the good qualities of the old school are his clarity, painstaking care of expression and, on the whole, an easy tranquillity of atmosphere. Much in his nature disposed to shape him as a poet of Classicism and, with occasional reserves, he is far more of a classical poet than a romantic. Yet throughout Cowper's work we feel from time to time a note of something that is certainly not the note of Pope or Dryden, something deeper in feeling than meets us even in Thomson, Collins, or Gray.

Certainly in his Nature-pictures there is a large measure of that healing power which John Stuart Mill found in Wordsworth. Lacking the vision of Wordsworth and his imaginative height, he is singularly like him in cool, peaceful, unforced magic.

The melancholia which affected his life gave a tinge of sadness, sometimes of terror, to his beautiful hymns, but could not darken the brightness of his human sympathies, and when, at times, the cloud lifted, there was a joyousness and light-heartedness about the man which found happy expression in his work.

His best poetry, in *The Task* and *The Winter Walk*, reflects the quiet, deliberate charm of " old haunted meadows " amid which he lived. He seemed to have absorbed into his being the homely charms of these rural parts, and his verse goes on its way with the leisurely rhythm of the slow-moving Ouse, neither grand nor varied, but gentle, persuasive, and soothing.

On the Receipt of My Mother's Picture

Oh, that those lips had language ! Life has pass'd
With me but roughly since I heard thee last.
Those lips are thine—thy own sweet smile I see,
The same that oft in childhood solaced me;
Voice only fails, else how distinct they say,
" Grieve not, my child, chase all thy fears away ! "
The meek intelligence of those dear eyes
(Blest be the art that can immortalize,
The art that baffles time's tyrannic claim
To quench it) here shines on me still the same.
Faithful remembrancer of one so dear,
Oh, welcome guest, though unexpected, here !
Who bidd'st me honour with an artless song,
Affectionate, a mother lost so long.

I will obey, not willingly alone,
But gladly, as the precept were her own;
And, while that face renews my filial grief,
Fancy shall weave a charm for my relief—
Shall steep me in Elysian reverie,
A momentary dream, that thou art she.

The Winter Walk at Noon

The night was winter in its roughest mood;
The morning sharp and clear.   But now at noon
Upon the southern side of the slant hills,
And where the woods fence off the northern blast,
The season smiles, resigning all its rage,
And has the warmth of May.   The vault is blue
Without a cloud, and white without a speck
The dazzling splendour of the scene below.
Again the harmony comes o'er the vale;
And through the trees I view th' embattled tow'r
Whence all the music.   I again perceive
The soothing influence of the wafted strains,
And settle in soft musings as I tread
The walk, still verdant, under oaks and elms,
Whose outspread branches overarch the glade.
The roof, though moveable through all its length
As the wind sways it, has yet well suffic'd,
And, intercepting in their silent fall
The frequent flakes, has kept a path for me.

George Crabbe was born in 1754, and brought up
among the simple fisher-folk of the village of Alde-
burgh in Suffolk, his father, a by no means gentle
parent, being a collector of salt dues.

During his apprenticeship to a surgeon he won a
magazine prize for his poem *Hope*, which turned him
towards literature as a profession.   Coming to London, he was nearer starvation than fame when Ed-

mund Burke acted the part of good Samaritan, and succeeded in getting his poem *The Library* published by Dodsley, in 1781. It was favourably noticed. Acting also on Burke's advice, he took Orders in 1781, his first curacy being in his native village; several livings were then offered to the man who was making a name for himself. Eventually he settled in Trowbridge, where he wrote *Tales of the Hall* (1818–19). In 1822 he journeyed to Edinburgh to visit Sir Walter Scott and, shortly after his return, he fell into ill-health. He died in 1832.

The Village was published in 1783, *The Parish Register* in 1803, and *The Borough* in 1810.

Horace Smith's well-known epithet concerning Crabbe, " a Pope in worsted stockings ", is no bad label. His frequent excursions with the couplet of Pope, his predilection for the epigrammatic line in which he sums up neatly a place, character, or person certainly suggests the Twickenham wit. But, with far less polish and dexterity of phrase, he transcends him immeasurably in passion and sincerity.

His own early hardships never embittered him but they give his picture of rural life a stern realism, a grim unloveliness which, while they occasionally depress and sometimes fatigue, are never lacking in interest. Whether in painting English life or English scenery, his method is the same, neither sentimental nor picturesque, yet always interesting from its sincerity and minute accuracy. There is nothing of the pensive sweetness and soothing beauty of Cowper's natural descriptions but a marked preference for the uncouth side of Nature. When treating human nature, he is more concerned with briars than with roses, with weeds than with blossom, with barren waste than with fertile meadows, and he invests them with an original force of minute description which compels our admiration.

Gipsies

                             On either side
Is level fen, a prospect wild and wide,
With dikes on either hand by ocean's self supplied :
Far on the right the distant sea is seen,
And salt the springs that feed the marsh between;
Beneath an ancient bridge the straitened flood
Rolls through its banks of slimy mud;
Near it a sunken boat resists the tide
That frets and hurries to th' opposite side;
The rushes sharp, that on borders grow,
Bend their brown flow'rets to the stream below,
Impure in all its course, in all its progress slow :
Here a grave Flora scarcely deigns to bloom,
Nor wears a rosy blush, nor sheds perfume :
The few dull flowers that o'er the place are spread
Partake the nature of their fenny bed;
Here on its wiry stem, in rigid bloom,
Grows the salt lavender that lacks perfume;
Here the dwarf sallows creep, the septfoil harsh,
And soft slimy mallow of the marsh;
Low on the ear the distant billows sound,
And just in view appears their stony bound;
No hedge or tree conceals the glowing sun;
Birds, save a wat'ry tribe, the district shun,
Nor chirp among the reeds where bitter waters run. . . .

Chapter Seven

Prose—Johnson to Sterne

(i) Samuel Johnson (1709–84) : Boswell

FOR nearly fifty years after the death of Pope, Johnson was the dominant figure in the literary life of the day. In his person he seemed at once an expression and a criticism of current social and ethical ideals. There is scarcely any phase of the life of his times which he does not touch with his forceful personality.

The son of a poor bookseller in Lichfield, he came up to London with twopence halfpenny in his pocket and a fragment of a play—little to aid him in his literary ambition. Fortunately he brought also an indomitable will and great powers of endurance.

The Johnson who lives for us today in the pages of Boswell is the successful Johnson, the literary dictator upon whose word everybody hung, the man who puts aside the author's craft with unmistakable satisfaction as soon as poverty could no longer dog his footsteps. But it is difficult to read aright the greatness or the weakness of the man unless we recall his early agonies in Grub Street.

Suffering hardens some natures, drying up the fount of pity and compassion. In Johnson's case it intensified the man's amazing tenderness of heart and deep-grained humanity; here it is that Johnson so far excels men like Addison and Pope. Addison's nature was sweeter and sounder than his rival's— graciousness, kindliness, and urbanity are certainly to be found in him. What one misses is that " divine discontent ", that riotous goodness of heart, that prodigal tenderness, which remain in our memories long after the roughness of Johnson is forgotten.

Dickens could never recall his youthful hardships save with fierce indignation; indelibly had his early sufferings seared his imagination; and Johnson would burst into tears when reminded of his dark days. One can well understand the meaning of his outburst : "No man but a blockhead ever wrote except for money ", and the intense relief with which he relinquished his pen. Boswell once expressed his wonder that Johnson had not more pleasure in writing than in not writing. " Sir," replied the irascible idol, " you may wonder."

Johnson started by writing for the *Gentleman's Magazine*—essays and reviews and a kind of parliamentary letter, where he took care " that the Whig dogs should not have the best of it ".

What first attracted attention to him was his poem *London*, published in 1738, written in the vein of Juvenal. This brought him ten guineas and the commendation of men like Pope, but little change in his general financial condition.

In 1744 appeared the life of his friend Richard Savage, a fine piece of biographical writing, despite its occasional unreliability. The success of this led to his being commissioned to prepare a *Dictionary of the English Language*, a work that occupied seven years. Johnson had little philological knowledge but he had a rich endowment of humour and sententious wisdom, and some of his definitions it would be hard to better from this standpoint. Occasionally his pet prejudices flaunt themselves rather freely, as in the unkind definition of oats as " a grain which in England is generally given to horses, but in Scotland supports the people ".

While he was plodding through this formidable task, he sought distraction in other matters. In 1749 appeared the *Vanity of Human Wishes*, while Garrick brought out the tragedy of *Irene*, which was partly written before Johnson had come up to London.

The play, though not successful, filled his impoverished exchequer by bringing him nearly £300.

Having essayed verse, dictionary-making, and the drama, Johnson turned to the essay, which was so popular a literary vehicle in his time.

The Rambler started its wanderings in the spring of 1750, and ran for two years. With the exception of a few contributions from Richardson, everything came freshly minted from the Doctor's mind.

The uniformity of style would have mattered less had Johnson not assumed so heavy and pedantic a manner. His last venture, *The Idler*, certainly drags its wheels less cumbrously, but in neither of these periodicals is Johnson seen at his best.

Rasselas, Prince of Abyssinia (1759) proved vastly more to the public taste. It is a curious and interesting book, tedious at times in Johnson's most elephantine style, but with flashes of happy description and a good deal of sound moralising on a variety of subjects.

After 1762 Johnson's skies cleared. A pension of £300 relieved him from the constant fear of poverty, and his mind ripened and brightened under his sunnier fortune. The famous " Literary Club " was established in 1764, to which Burke, Goldsmith, Garrick, Gibbon, and Reynolds belonged. Here Johnson reigned as dictator.

At twelve o'clock, we are told, he received a levee of morning visitors in his bedroom—Goldsmith and others, chiefly men of letters—and to them he would declaim over a twelve-o'clock dish of tea. He then went to dinner at a tavern, most frequently the Mitre Tavern, where he commonly stayed late, and afterwards drank his tea at a friend's house, over which he loitered a great deal, but seldom took supper. He frequently gave all the silver in his pocket to the poor, who watched him between his house and the tavern where he dined.

Johnson had not altogether eschewed the author's craft; indeed, his best work was yet to come; but his literary output at no time gave a commensurate idea of the abilities of the man. His Shakespearean criticism reveals more of the author's limitations than the greatness of his subject. *The Journey to the Western Isles of Scotland* is certainly amusing, though largely as a piece of self-revelation. His most considerable production, *The Lives of the Poets* (1779–81), despite its incompleteness and occasionally glaring insensibilities—as in his treatment of Gray and Milton—contains some admirable critical appreciations.

In 1775 he received his doctor's degree from Oxford and was at the height of his popularity and influence. But the indifferent health which had dogged him all his life now began to make more encroachments. When, during the last year or so, he was without the society of his friend Mrs. Thrale, his spirits declined and his health grew rapidly worse.

But he had many faithful friends, including Burke and Reynolds, who tried to make his last days easy; and, irascible and impatient as Johnson had been by temperament, he showed singular endurance and resignation during his fatal illness. On December 13, 1784, he died, and was buried in Westminster Abbey.

James Boswell (1740–95) was born in Edinburgh, his father being an able advocate at the Scottish Bar and an uncompromising Presbyterian Whig. James was " a fine boy, wore a white cockade, and prayed for James King until his Uncle Cochrane gave him a shilling to pray for King George, which he accordingly did ". This accommodating youth studied law for a while, somewhat reluctantly, philosophy and rhetoric perhaps less reluctantly, and the wild Bohemian life of Edinburgh with no reluctance whatever. Coming up to London in 1760, he found pleasanter distractions from legal studies than he had done in Scotland;

despite an excursion into verse, *The Cub at Newmarket*, he showed no marked propensity for either the letters or law. Then, happily both for himself and posterity, Tom Davies, in Goldsmith's words, " flung him at Johnson in sport ", and he found his true vocation. " Who is this Scotch cur at Johnson's heels ? " asked someone of Goldsmith. " He is not a cur; he is only a bur," was the happy response. Indeed, had it not been for the " bur ", how little we might know of the man Johnson to-day !

The Doctor did not take kindly to his enthusiastic worshipper at first, but soon they became great friends and remained so for life, despite the irritability of the hero of the times. " Sir, you appear to have only two subjects : yourself and me, and I am sick of both."

No man of letters was ever more naïve than Boswell ; here he transcends even Pepys, yet his *naïveté*, his stupidities, drew out the gruff Doctor as no intellectual cunning could have done. And if Boswell stands revealed as a somewhat contemptible and certainly foolish personage in the pages of the biography, yet he cannot be written down as a fool. He had a wonderful memory and a natural instinct for presenting his material dramatically and vividly. No mere fool could have written the *Life of Samuel Johnson* : he was a fool of genius, for the biography is one of the great biographies of literature.

Johnson never wrote better than when under the influence of some powerful human emotion. When his inspiration is wholly literary he is apt to grow pompous and pedantic with alarming speed; when, however, some human concern projects itself into his work, then he shakes off his stiffness and writes with force and dignity.

In his *Life of Savage*, his criticism of Pope and Dryden, his picture of life in the Happy Valley in *Rasselas*, Johnson touches on some chord of memory or peculiar mental affinity that bares him for us at his best and finest.

Johnson, however, lives for most of us in the pages of Boswell, rather than in his own writings; and for this reason. Clearly as some of his characteristics reveal themselves to us in his work, he found the freest self-expression in " talk ". He had a craggy mind which kept in admirable condition when rubbed against other minds. And no mind was better calculated to educe its sharp and solid qualities of cragginess than Boswell's. Boswell's pages exhibit the splendid inconsistencies of the man, his gigantic prejudices and conventionalities, and the equally colossal breadth of his moral sympathies; his dense stupidity on some points, such as the value of public executions, and amazing good sense on others; his mingled melancholy and cheerfulness, his intellectual timidity and unconquerable courage. Give him a pen and he tried to be judicial, which nature had taken good care he should never be; hear him talk, and you found the tonic of his fundamental common-sense behind his most monstrous extravagances.

This, however, does not mean that his writings are negligible. It only means that they are of secondary account, and are best studied after Boswell. By interpreting him first of all through Boswell's pages, we shall best value the sturdy humour and sagacity that lie embedded in the *Dictionary*, the flashes of insight that illuminate the prolix *Lives of the Poets*, and the touches of tenderness and poetry that light up the often dismal moralising of *Rasselas*.

Vanity of Human Wishes

Let Observation, with extensive view,
Survey mankind from China to Peru;
Remark each anxious toil, each eager strife,
And watch the busy scenes of crowded life;
Then say, how hope and fear, desire and hate,
O'erspread with snares the clouded maze of fate,
Where wavering man, betray'd by vent'rous pride
To tread the dreary paths without a guide,
As treacherous phantoms in the mist delude,
Shuns fancied ills, or chases airy good;
How rarely reason guides the stubborn choice,
Rules the bold hand, or prompts the suppliant voice;
How nations sink, by darling schemes oppress'd,
When Vengeance listens to the fool's request;
Fate wings with every wish th' afflictive dart,
Each gift of nature, and each grace of art;
With fatal heat impetuous courage glows,
With fatal sweetness elocution flows;
Impeachment stops the speaker's powerful breath,
And restless fire precipitates on death.

(ii) Oliver Goldsmith (1728–74)

Oliver Goldsmith was born in County Longford, Ireland, in 1728, his father being a " Curate farmer ", the Rev. Charles Goldsmith, and his mother the schoolmaster's daughter. The Rev. Charles received £40 a year, " a fortune which he brought five children into the world to share ".

Oliver was the fifth child, a slow, ugly, and ungainly boy. At the village school he learned a good deal about ghosts and fairies—little else. Later on (1744), at Trinity College, Dublin, he was still unconcerned with learning, though he just managed to take his degree, and his earlier years may be epitomised in one word—failure.

With light-hearted exuberance he tried the Church, the Bar, Medicine, in rapid succession, and showed brilliant incompetence in each. His only real success, perhaps, was his invention of street ballads at five shillings each, and his most poignant delight at this time was hearing them sung under an oil lamp.

His father died in 1749 and Oliver was cast on his own resources, which were uncommonly tenuous. He started to emigrate to America with £30, but never sailed, as he was " at a pleasure party " at the time, where he lost all his money as well as the boat. Then he essayed the Law and his uncle encouraged him with £50—a sum that was promptly wasted in a Dublin gaming-house. Afterwards, at Edinburgh, he applied himself for a while to chemistry and natural history; then the vagrant spirit seized him again; he went abroad with a smattering of medical knowledge, twenty pounds, and a flute.

Borrowing money for his journey, he characteristic-

ally spent it at the start on a preposterous gift of tulip
bulbs for his kindly uncle, then footed it through
Flanders, France, and Switzerland, relying on his
flute to provide him with supper and bed. Yet he
was never really downhearted, and observed signi-
ficantly " that he found people sprightly in proportion
to their wants, and the poorer often the sprightlier ".

For, to tell the truth, he was a genuine vagabond
at heart, with that itch of restlessness in the blood
which made him an alien to the comfortable jog-trot
conventions of civilised life. He was really predestined
for poverty, not merely because he found it so hard
to make money but because, even having made it, he
was quite unable to keep it.

On his return from abroad in 1756 he became in
turn an usher, a printer's reader, a reviewer, and a
bookseller's hack; and at the age of thirty was living
in miserable rooms at Ludgate Lane, writing social
sketches, making translations, and trying his hand at a
history of England. Unreliable and ignorant as he
often was in his miscellaneous hack-writing, he was
never dull, and very soon the fine originality of the
man and his native grace of style showed themselves.

He started the *Bee*, a short-lived paper, with a good
deal of excellent essay work in it, and wrote *The Citizen
of the World*. *The Traveller* appeared in 1764, and at
this time he was on intimate terms with Johnson's
circle.

During one of Goldsmith's financial crises, Johnson
rescued him with a guinea, finding the sheriff's officer

in possession. Naturally, Goldsmith spent the guinea on Madeira. Johnson "put the cork in the bottle, desiring he would be calm"; Goldsmith then showed him a manuscript—*The Vicar of Wakefield.* Johnson was struck by its merits and, according to his own account, sold it to a bookseller for £60. *The Vicar* brought Goldsmith fame—more important than money, for money was never his for long. Following *The Vicar of Wakefield* came *The Good-Natured Man,* his first play; *The Deserted Village,* that showed him as a poet of no mean order; and his best comedy, *She Stoops to Conquer.* Then in 1774 he died, worn out, of a fever, in material squalor and mental misery, but mourned and beloved by many friends.

Characteristics

(a) *Whimsicality.*—In Goldsmith's temperament melancholy and mirth lay cheek by jowl, antagonistic comrades, one would think, but not unusual in the spiritual composition of imaginative men. Melancholy was for ever trying to drag him down, and did succeed in making him often tongue-tied and wistful, but careless and happy-go-lucky gaiety broke through all the barriers from time to time, unexpectedly, disconcertingly, the more wild and ebullient for the repression.

Indeed, his quaint whimsicality, passing unexpectedly from delicate fancy to elfish merriment, anticipates in many ways the methods of *Elia* and Leigh Hunt. His prose-writing, therefore, is of special interest to the modern student of the Essay. He was a poet of talent, a proseman of genius—a proseman, moreover, of distinctive and original genius. With no scholarly equipment, with little opportunity to indulge his fanciful imagination to the full, working always under heavy disabilities, he has none the less a native instinct for the sweet and gracious things of life, and a clear, limpid, delicate style for expressing them.

Consider, moreover, those inimitable touches which make of *The Vicar of Wakefield*—a thin, unsatisfactory story, judged strictly as a piece of fiction—one of the classics. When we think of this book, memory lingers less on the artless plot, or even the central figure of the genial, kind-hearted Vicar, than upon the cousins " even to the fourteenth remove " who came to eat his dinners and borrow his books; on the wife who had made of pickles and preserving a fine art, and discoursed at dinner on the history of every dish; on Moses disposing of the pony for a gross of green spectacles. The moral qualities of Primrose attract us far less than do his foibles, his peculiar method of cheering his wife by writing her epitaph and putting it up over the mantelpiece.

How admirable are such descriptive passages as this :

" Our little habitation was situated at the foot of a sloping hill, sheltered with a beautiful underwood behind, and a prattling river before; on one side a meadow, on the other a green. . . . One story covered with thatch, which gave it an air of great snugness; the walls on the inside were nicely whitewashed . . . though the same room served for parlour and kitchen . . . that only made it the warmer. Besides, as it was kept with the utmost neatness, the dishes, plates and copper, being well scoured, all disposed in bright rows on the shelves, the eye was agreeably relieved, and did not want richer furniture."

(b) *His Tenderness.*—Allied with whimsicality is a tenderness of heart which found also full expression in his work. His sentimentality is equal to the best in Richardson and Sterne, and is cleaner and saner; for his sense of humour never allows him to become mawkish.

It has been well said of him that charity was his one luxury. Not with all the buffeting he suffered from Fate was he ever spiteful—this, too, in an age when bitter things were flung about so readily by the humorist of the day.

Yet he was fully alive to the defects of his companions and friends, but when he touches on them, he does so lightly, gracefully, tenderly, with no particle of malice.

Easy-going and good-hearted to a fault as he was, he could be inflexible as steel where principles were concerned.

What Goldsmith did for literature, whether in prose, verse, or drama, was to sweeten and purify it from its violence, coarseness, and bitter wit. He had not the great driving force of Swift and Defoe, the exquisite polish of Pope, the dominating personality of Johnson, or the grasp of character and ebullient diversity of some of his great contemporaries of fiction, yet he has qualities especially his own—a tranquil magic, a tender homeliness, a light, iridescent humour that will ever endear him to posterity.

(iii) Samuel Richardson (1689–1761)

A fat, tubby, mild-looking, smooth-cheeked, ruddy-faced, little man, guiltless of any external graces; this is the man who became the idol of his day during the earlier years of the eighteenth century—one who moved in a little crowd of female worshippers eager to render him the constant tribute of their tears.

He was a rigid moralist in the day when loose living was the rule rather than the exception; a loyal abstainer in an age when it was considered almost a point of etiquette to round off your dinner on the floor; a vegetarian when dietary reform was looked on as a dangerous form of mental affection. If we turn from this general view of his personality and recall his history, we shall see how entirely it harmonises with the man as we know him.

Born in 1689, in Derbyshire, the son of a London joiner, he was at first intended for Holy Orders but, not obtaining the necessary advantages of a good education, he was apprenticed at the age of seventeen to an Aldersgate printer, John Wilde. Earnest and plodding from his early days, he applied himself to the work like one of the good little boys in his own didactic fiction and, like Hogarth's "industrious apprentice ", married his master's daughter, becoming a master printer himself in 1719.

The exciting diversion of making indices and writing dedications varied his professional work. He wrote a few novels, made money, took to himself a " country house " at Fulham, became printer of the *Journal* of the House of Commons, Master of the Stationer's Company, and Law Printer to the King. Then, in the odour of respectability, he died on July 4, 1761, being buried in St. Bride's Church, Fleet Street, close to his old shop (no longer existent), No. 11 Salisbury Court.

His wife died in 1731, before he had achieved any literary fame; then came *Pamela, or Virtue Rewarded*, in 1740—his first fiction and one that scored an instant and signal success.

Encouraged by its reception, he issued a volume of *Familiar Letters* in 1741.

The interest excited by *Pamela* was fully sustained by *Clarissa Harlowe*. Both books have one element in common. Each deals with a matter that has never failed to attract readers of fiction or spectators of melodrama—the picture of a girl struggling against adverse fate. *Pamela* gives us a young girl in lowly life, pressed by the dishonourable attentions of her employer's son; *Clarissa* portrays a girl, in better material circumstances, in love with a scapegrace. In neither case is there anything to be said in favour of the gentleman, but whereas Pamela's affection seems largely a matter of shrewd calculation and worldly wisdom, that of Clarissa, however misguided, is genuine enough.

In both cases we are faced with much the same problem—the struggle between environment and character. Circumstances say, " Do this ! " Morality says, " Do that ! " Which will prevail ? Will the woman succumb to temptation, or prove mistress of her fate ?

Pamela solves the problem by insisting on marriage with her good-for-nothing but well-to-do lover. He marries her; thus is Virtue Rewarded. Clarissa holds out against the worthless Lovelace, finally dying of grief, and shaming him by her death into some sense of his blackguardly conduct.

Clarissa is not merely a more attractive character than Pamela; she is more carefully and subtly drawn, and her appeal to the reader's sympathies more comprehensible. The end to Pamela is—bathos; there is real pathos in Clarissa's death. Pamela's lover is a dull lay figure. Lovelace, perhaps, is also a lay figure, but he is not a dull one. If not alive, the puppet at any rate is smartly dressed.

So firm an affection did Clarissa rouse in her readers that the veteran Colley Cibber swore " if she should die he would no longer believe in Providence ".

Clarissa was followed by *Sir Charles Grandison*. Hitherto his chief characters had been women. Someone had persuaded him to try his hand at a model gentleman, and Grandison is the result.

Placed beside that admirable picture of the

eighteenth-century courtly knight, Sir Roger de Coverley, his limitations are obvious enough. Coverley is lovable, with his ripe geniality and quaint tenderness. Grandison, eschewing human frailties, succeeds merely in shaping as a dreadful prig. Yet, for all that, he is no lay figure. He strikes one as the stiff, eighteenth-century prototype of the redoubtable Sir Willoughby Patterne. Meredith drew his men in the spirit of mocking irony; Richardson in the spirit of admiring didacticism. The result is not wholly dissimilar. Each is profoundly self-centred, artificial, and prosy to the core, with many external graces and accomplishments. For this reason probably, he may interest the modern reader, despite his exasperating "uprightness", certainly not exactly as intended by Richardson, but because he does, in his way, give us a certain type of man.

Richardson's house in the North End Road, Fulham, was crowded by worshippers at this time, and we have a picture of the plump little author wearing a velvet cap and dressing-gown, with one hand on his heart, the other holding a copy of *Grandison*, reading aloud to his admirers in the garden.

Characteristics

(a) *The Sentimental Note*.—Sentimentality is one of the big stage properties of romance and, because of its almost universal appeal, romance was dearly loved for many centuries. With the advent of realism into fiction, sentimentality bulked far less prominently.

Neither Greene nor Nash discarded it, but the effort
to induce actuality into fiction led necessarily to a
method which considered other matters than a constant appeal to the emotions.   In Defoe it is at a mini-
mum.   He was by temperament neither fanciful nor
emotional, and the absence of sentiment in his writing
is, from the point of view of the popular novelist, his
most notable defect.

Richardson's enormous popularity is due to the
fact that he recognised the part played in everyday life
by sentiment, and he gave his readers sentiment
enough to please the most emotional of them.   His
deliberate, minute, detailed method enabled him to
give the utmost effect to the sentimental note.   To-
day we are not moved by discursive sentimentalising
to a like extent, though even now the sentimental
writer may always reckon on a large audience; but
in those days, when sentiment was tabooed in verse,
a generous supply of it in fiction proved especially
acceptable.   It is a mistake to speak, as we sometimes
do, of the formal, unemotional eighteenth century;
it is an estimate based entirely on its leading school of
poetry.   People at large were fully as prone to sentiment, as fond of sentiment, then as now.   Literary
fashions may change, but human nature remains
pretty constant from century to century; and the
absence of sentiment and passion in the verse of the
day merely served to exaggerate its expression in the
fiction of the time.

Richardson's method is cumulative.   For instance,

in *Pamela* each letter is rather more harrowing than the one preceding; in *Clarissa* each scene more poignant until the climax is reached.

(b) *The Characterisation.*—Some writers, like Defoe, paint their characters with an economy of touches (for Defoe's power of detail is exerted to elucidate his "incidents", and the probabilities of his stories, not his "personages" and their fidelity to life). Others, such as Richardson, build up their characters slowly— touch by touch and line by line, so that they gradually assume stereoscopic substantiality. We learn about them from their own speeches and behaviour, and from what others say about them. Thus it is that, despite the astounding prolixity of the author, he does achieve his purpose, in impressing upon the imagination a story with some real characters in it. No doubt there is a good deal that might be spared, trivialities of gossip that do not further any valuable purpose, such as the names of the persons who went in the separate coaches on the occasion of Grandison's wedding, or the exact amount of money that Sir Charles gave to the village girls who decked the pathway with flowers, but he leaves out no detail of importance in filling up the full-length portraits.

This does not imply, of course, that Richardson is uniformly successful in his characterisation. On the contrary, he is remarkably circumscribed. But when he knows his character, he has the art of making us know the person also. Women, with their subtleties and inconsistencies, he can depict with extraordinary skill, and for the first time in the history of English fiction we have the woman's point of view. This power of portraying women is often seen among the dramatists, especially the Elizabethans; but no Elizabethan novelist showed any special faculty in this direction, and Defoe was great enough to realise his limitations here.

Richardson, therefore, is not only our first novelist of character, but our first depictor of feminine character. Pamela may not be the sweet and virtuous maiden Richardson tried to make us think she is, but that is because the conventional moralist in him blinds the author to the significance of those masterly touches by which he himself places the character of this crafty little minx before us. Clarissa also, seen through the prismatic glory of her creator's tears, fails to convince us of her supreme claims to moral excellence, but she does undoubtedly convince us of her reality as a certain type of woman, with her life-like vacillations, her mingled obstinacy and weakness, and such delightful touches as the tearing of Lovelace's ruffles. In his third novel Grandison takes the central place and the women are more sketchily drawn, yet the two girls, Harriet Byron and Clementi, are cleverly differentiated and are by no means puppets.

Of the men one must speak with greater reserve. Lovelace has found vigorous defenders, and it may well be true that Richardson knew the male villain fairly intimately; but intimacy with a scoundrel gives no guarantee of artistic power to depict that scoundrel.

My own view is that Richardson's temperament was largely feminine, his standpoint on life almost entirely feminine, and that, where he did succeed with his male characters, it was in those feminine aspects that are to be found in men no less than in women.

Lovelace is really a woman's rake tempered by the moralist; Grandison is a woman's " gentleman ". Virile humanity was quite beyond Richardson's reach, but feminine element in man Richardson could always suggest.

(c) *Morality*.—" There is always something ", remarked Dr. Johnson, " which Clarissa preferred to truth." Johnson was a great, though disconcerting, admirer of the novelist and here he certainly strikes on the real weakness in Richardson's moral outlook. He valued himself upon the morality of his pieces; never relinquished the pulpit attitude; yet the morality, when analysed, is often found to be nothing better than discreet opportunism. Pamela, as we have seen, was a designing little madam, and Clarissa, certainly his finest creation, has no vital strength of character or nobility of soul. She is chaste, sensitive, and sympathetic; when we have said that we have said all. She does not belong to the highest type of womanhood.

Yet Richardson not only took himself seriously as a novelist and classed his fiction with such books as Taylor's *Holy Living* and *The Whole Duty of Man*, but was esteemed by most of his contemporaries as a profound teacher.

The morality of Richardson is the morality of his age; not salted by tolerant humour, as in Fielding's case, but often sentimentalised to an unhealthy extent. "If you were to read Richardson for the story", said Johnson in an oft-quoted passage, "your impatience would be so much fretted, you would hang yourself." It might well be said today that if you read him for his morality you deserve someone else to hang you.

Johnson counselled us to read him for his sentiment. The modern reader would prefer, no doubt, and with good reason, to read him for his power of delineation, and for a literary style that, despite its prolixity and involutions, is yet singularly effective.

Richardson introduced sentimentality into English fiction and popularised it for ever. Without his influence we might never have had *Tristram Shandy*; we certainly would have been without *Joseph Andrews*; and ill could we have afforded to lose these novels. Then the feminine standpoint taken in his writings stirred many able women to continue and amplify the feminine tradition. Fanny Burney and Jane Austen, and a host of lesser names, are indebted to him.

These things must be remembered when we shudder at his moralising, laugh at his absurdities, and yawn over his interminable length. He is the first novelist to show a real and vital knowledge of the human heart, its perversities and contradictions—the first to analyse the woman's point of view; and the man who did that deserves some measure of praise from posterity.

(iv) Henry Fielding (1707-54)

In person, disposition, and pedigree, Henry Fielding presents a remarkable contrast to his famous contemporary.   In the first place, he was an aristocrat, the " House of Fielding " claiming kinship with that of Hapsburg and dating from the twelfth century. His great-grandfather was the first Earl of Desmond, his grandfather Canon of Salisbury, his father one of Marlborough's generals.   On the mother's side, his grandfather was a Justice of the King's Bench, and Lady Mary Worley Montagu was his cousin.

Fielding was good-looking, tall, and well-made, with abundant animal spirits, a fine wit, and an open, genial disposition, one well calculated to attract a host of friends.   One thing only, and that no unusual one, tempered the young man's satisfaction in life— the poverty of his patrimony.

Born at Sharpham Park, near Glastonbury, in 1707, he was educated for Eton by a Mr. Oliver, who " could have acted the part of Falstaff without stuffing ", and was noted for " a stateliness in his gait when he walked not unlike that of a goose, only if he stalked the slower ".

After leaving Eton, maybe in reaction against book-study, he planned an elopement with a Miss Sarah Andrews but this, owing to his guardian's care, remained merely a pious aspiration.   After journeying to Leyden to study law, he became embarrassed by his father's forgetfulness in the matter of an allowance, so he returned to London, resolved to see what his own wits could do for him.

The most obvious lucrative business in those days for a young man of parts was playwriting, and the young wit wasted little time in getting to work.

Love in Several Masques was produced in 1728, and a host of others quickly followed; the majority fairly successful but none of them having much merit save the amusing *Tragedy of Tragedies; or The Life and Death of Tom Thumb the Great* (1731), in which he parodied agreeably the mannerisms of Lee and Rowe. Another of them, *Don Quixote in England*, is worth recording, since it contained that typical English song, " The Roast Beef of Old England ".

The playwright then made drama on his own account; he fell in love with a Miss Charlotte Craddock, a beautiful, wealthy, and accomplished lady who lived at Salisbury. For her he waited four years, during which time the course of true love underwent many exciting vicissitudes. Then, in 1735, he tired of play-writing, not because of financial failure in that direction, for he had done well from a material point of view, but because he realised that the drama gave him no proper scope for his own literary gifts. Political satire interested him for a while, then he turned to the Bar, and while there was attracted by the sensational success of *Pamela*. In 1742 he planned and executed what was, in inception and form, a parody of Richardson's book, but was in essence a fresh stage in the development of the novel. Fielding was then thirty-five.

Encouraged by its success, he published, in 1743, three volumes of *Miscellanies*, including one of the finest pieces of ironical fiction in the language, *Jonathan Wild*. Then for a while he devoted himself to Whig journalism, writing the *True Patriot* and the *Jacobite Journal*; and in 1749 published his most popular novel, *Tom Jones*. Meanwhile his wife had died and the author had become a Bow Street magistrate. While performing his duties here—which he did with vigour and admirable sense—he found time to produce *Amelia* in 1751, and to conduct for some time the *Covent Garden Journal*. His health broke down and he travelled abroad, hoping to restore it. Fielding's vitality, however, had been sapped, and he died in October 1754, at Lisbon. After his death his last book, *A Voyage to Lisbon*, was published.

When Fielding planned out *Joseph Andrews*, on the modest lines of a burlesque, he had not reckoned on his creative imagination and on Parson Adams. In Chapter XI the worthy parson appears and takes the story into his own hands. It ceases to become a satire on the novel of morals and becomes a pioneer of the novel of manners. Here we have the dividing line between Richardson and Fielding as novelists. Fielding in his own way is also a pronounced moralist. But he is a painter of manners first, and Richardson was first a moralist.

Jonathan Wild (1743) reveals Fielding in another

light. There is nothing here of the robust satirical humour of the novels, nothing of the discursive moralising, little of the social historian. It is a grim and powerful piece of ironic portraiture, showing on heroic scale the villainies of the highwayman, and wrought with an artistic skill and clarity of purpose that it would be hard to over-praise. The underlying thesis, indeed, is a kind of anticipation of De Quincey's brilliant *Murder as One of the Fine Arts*. The feature that unites *Jonathan Wild* with the novels is the vitality of the characterisation, great and small.

But the flavour of *Jonathan Wild* is too subtle, too bitter for some palates, and *Tom Jones* is certainly to the taste of most people. Like Kipling's Tommy, Tom Jones " ain't no bloomin' 'ero ", and in his anxiety to emphasise his humanity Fielding seems—to the modern reader, at any rate—to have drawn rather a too ordinary " young man about town ". But if Tom himself is not a particularly attractive scapegrace, there are many characters who are welcome. Good-natured Allworthy is by no means insipid, as he might easily have been; Black George is a vigorously vital rascal; Partridge is amusing company, and Squire Western an irresistible picture of the " three-bottle " country gentleman. The real villains and humbugs (hot-blooded villainy Fielding can always condone) are somewhat too villainous to convince us; but if we find Blifil too monstrous to stomach, there is the breezy exuberance and liveliness of the storytelling by way of compensation.

Amelia, his third novel, is the fruit of his later years, and reflects Fielding as the critic of legal administration and our social machinery. The buoyancy of his early method is replaced by a graver, maturer style, as befitted one who had learned much of contemporary life on its seamy side while a magistrate. There is less humour, less gaiety, less diversity than before, but in the more serious passages Fielding is at his happiest. None of his women characters has the grace and sweetness of Amelia. She is drawn from life, and in her the novelist paints, with tender fidelity and with the delicate insight born of love and knowledge, the charms of womanly woman, devoid of the sugary namby-pambyism that Richardson could never resist, and of the conventional touches that make Sophia Western never anything more than a pretty shadow.

Characteristics

(a) *His Satiric Humour.*—The society that Fielding painted was a coarse and noisy one, but Fielding draws attention to the fact that " its bark is worse than its bite ", that it is more frivolous and thoughtless than deliberately bad. His genial humour playing over its rough surface easily and spaciously irradiates everyone who is not a hypocrite or a muff. The essential humanity of his characters is their most attractive asset, and this it is that gives such astonishing vitality to his work. His treatment of hypocrisy is the least satisfactory illustration of his art, for his hearty detestation of it prevents him from making his hypocrites plausible.

One can well understand how his rich humour delighted Dickens and stimulated him to create like portraits of his own—portraits often more ludicrous but not more actual. Certainly, the character of Parson Adams alone justified John Forster's comment on Fielding's habit of " discerning what was good and beautiful in the homeliest aspects of humanity ".

The precise value of Fielding's moral attitude towards life may be disregarded for the moment. Even apart from that, it is quite easy to understand the feud between him and Richardson. Richardson's immense solemnity precludes the faintest ray of humour. The modern reader may often smile in reading his pages, but it is at the author, not with him. Fielding, with a more diverse experience of human life, and with a gaiety of temperament which even in mellower years never quite lost its buoyancy, treats his story and his characters always from the point of view of the humorist not in the least anxious to hide the weaknesses and idiosyncrasies, rejoicing in them rather, and feeling decidedly more comfortable when he can have a good laugh at his hero.

But there is a great and notable exception to the general run of Fielding's humour. That exception is found in *Jonathan Wild*. As an imaginative picture of ordinary human life the book is inferior to its predecessor and successor, but as an intellectual presentment in the guise of fiction of a genus of the human species it stands easily first as a masterly essay in ironic humour, claiming kinship with the mordant genius of *The Tale of a Tub* and *Candide*. Perhaps it is Fielding's greatest achievement in literature; certainly it is one of the great books of the century.

If Parson Adams illustrated the sympathetic quality of Fielding's humour, and Jonathan Wild its intellectual power, Squire Western affords us one of the happiest examples of its moral sensibility. Western is a coarse, violent, domineering man, astonishingly actual and, for all his grossness, never wholly repulsive. Deep down in his sensual nature, and below his fierce intolerance, there is a strain of tenderness and good-heartedness.

(b) *His Common-sense Morality.*—From the very first it is clear that Fielding is resolved to tilt against the cloying sentimentality brought into vogue by Richardson's *Pamela*. In *Joseph Andrews* he burlesqued this mawkish ideal, giving us in Abraham Adams a picture of the genuine sentiment for which he cared. This pursuit of current heroics he carries into *Jonathan Wild*, stripping the picturesque trappings off the " popular " rogue, and displaying him in all his ugliness and brutality. It is quite clear, therefore, that Fielding's attitude was not merely a negative one ; his object was to replace a morbid by a healthy, common-sense morality.

The moral intent, indeed, was obvious in his plays, when he first began to satirise the follies of the day; and this is coupled with an equally vigorous intention

of enjoying life to the full.   He frowns on all attempts
to wave away the " cakes and ale ", merely postulating
that the cakes should be well baked and the ale sound
and wholesome.

If you sup too freely of them, then you must put up
with the consequences, Fielding seems to say.   If he
regards intemperance of living with too indulgent an
eye, we must recollect the general tone of his day.
The " wild-oats " theory was accepted as a necessary
step in life.   Fielding's coarseness, however, is all
above-board.   It may be rank, but it is quite honest
and straightforward.   He may tolerate it; but he
makes no attempt to gloss it.   Richardson recognised
the animalism and called it high-falutin' names;
Fielding frankly accepted it;   man is an animal,
according to him, and there is no use disguising the
animalism; but he is something more.

This common-sense morality, combined with his
satiric humour, gave him a shrewd insight into the
weaknesses of his characters.   Admirable, for instance,
is the sketch of Mrs. James in *Amelia*.   Here she is
writing about the heroine :

> " In the first place her eyes were too large and she hath
> a look with them, that I don't know how to describe;
> but I know I don't like it.   Then her eyebrows are too
> large, indeed she doth all in her power to remedy this
> with pincers, for if it was not for those her eyebrows
> would be preposterous.   Then her nose . . . scar
> on one side.   Neck too protuberant for the genteel
> size, especially as she laces herself . . . Lastly, both
> too short and too tall.   Well, you may laugh, Mr.

James, I know what I mean though I cannot well express it. I mean she is too tall for a pretty woman, and too short for a fine woman. . . ."

(v) Tobias Smollett (1721–71)

Born in 1721, at Dalquhurn House in the west of Scotland, of good stock, young Smollett could boast no better patrimony than had his contemporary, Fielding. Like him he received a good education, and was then apprenticed to a surgeon in Glasgow. But his heart lay in books, not in bottles, and 1739 saw him in London, with a drama on James I of Scotland in his pocket and all sorts of wild dreams in his head. Fortune failed to smile on him, however, so he found employment for five years as a surgeon's mate on board a king's ship, during the war with Spain.

His experiences there stood him in good stead, for during these five years he may be said to have served his apprenticeship to literature. On his return, with Scottish shrewdness he married a woman with money, but being (as Fielding was not) very extravagant, he speedily ran through it. Once again he tried his fortune as a surgeon, but his volatile, impetuous temperament did not inspire patients with confidence. No one had seemed anxious to encourage him as a writer of tragedy, so he turned now to satire, *Advice* and *The Reproof* (1745). These faring little better, he bethought him of fiction, made use of his youthful experiences, and offered the public *The Adventures of Roderick Random*.

This novel is frankly an imitation of the picaresque Spanish fiction *Gil Blas*; it caught the public taste, by its liveliness and freshness. *Peregrine Pickle* followed in 1751, also *The Adventures of Ferdinand, Count Fathom* (1753), a poor and ineffective satire on the lines of *Jonathan Wild*. His last novel, *The Expedition of Humphrey Clinker*, was finished in Leghorn and published a few days before his death in 1771.

As a writer Smollett could boast a lively and vivid style. His stories are rich in incident, there is abundant " go " in them and, though very unequal in characterisation, this gift of telling a good yarn prevents him from being dull. Of his three novels, *Peregrine Pickle* is the freshest and most diversified, *Humphrey Clinker* the mellowest.

But the greatest claim that Smollett has on our consideration is his genius for depicting oddities. Generally speaking, he is on a lower level as a literary artist than either Richardson or Fielding. He has not a tithe of Richardson's psychological subtlety, nor has his vision the sanity and diversity of Fielding's. But in the creation of oddities he is certainly easily first.

His seamen are the real thing : they have the salt savour of the sea about them and are a real and valuable contribution to the portrait-gallery of fiction. Here he draws upon his own experiences; he can paint the sea-rover, for he himself has been a sea-rover; and the reader can visualise easily every hole and cranny on board H.M.S. *Thunder*; while that remarkable decoction " bumbo "—rum, sugar-water, and nutmeg—is not easily forgotten. Hatchway and Pipes are the humorous and vital figures who impress the memory. That they lapse into caricature from time to time is certainly true. But, as with many of Dickens's characters, they are described with such infinite zest, with such huge and obvious enjoyment, that the hilarious contagion spreads to the reader.

Personally Smollett was a man of fiery temper and strong prejudices, with a decided forcefulness of character and an aggressive goodness of heart that seemed to say at times, " If you won't let me do you a service I'll jolly well punch your head ! " There is in his work much of that fresh exuberance that we find in Fielding, with greater coarseness and less urbanity, but to the reader with a relish for farce there is certainly much enjoyment to be found in the rollicking extravagances so abundant in the novels.

In experience of life Fielding and Smollett are about equal. Both knew the vagabond pretty thoroughly, whether as swaggering adventurer or as a " lady without reputation "; while against Fielding's superior knowledge of better-class society in town and country may be placed Smollett's knowledge of the sea-rover and his more extensive experience of other countries.

Very popular in his day, with both the women and the men, his reputation has during the present century declined. If Scott's enthusiastic eulogy errs on the side of over-praise, the verdict of the present generation seems to err on the other side.

Smollett had serious limitations as a story-teller, but when all his defects are duly admitted this much may be said of him: he invented a new type of character, made possible the creation of Captain Cuttle, inspired Marryat, and Thackeray probably in his Barry Lyndon; while his influence lingers yet in the drolleries of W. W. Jacobs. And this is no poor recommendation.

(vi) Laurence Sterne (1713–68)

Born in 1713 at Clonmel, Ireland, Laurence was the son of a poor lieutenant, Roger Sterne. His early days were spent at York, Dublin, Liverpool, and Plymouth, and his vicissitudes then, especially the memory of his good-hearted, easy-going father, served him in good stead when he started to write.

After taking his degree at Cambridge he became a priest, and obtained by avuncular patronage a living at Coxwold, near York.

His spiritual qualifications were slight, but these were not looked for at that time. Of his preaching powers there is a legend that, when occasionally he ascended the pulpit at York Minster, " half the congregation left the church, as delivery and voice proved so disagreeable ".

However, if his clerical gifts were inconsiderable, he had other qualifications not amiss in a country gentleman. He was a good shot, read, fiddled, and painted, and as he had taken the precaution to marry " a homely woman with a fortune " one may judge that he passed

his time pleasantly enough.   How far he satisfied his
flock is another matter.

A rector who would, when going to church, suddenly
return home for his gun on espying a covey of part-
ridges must have proved somewhat trying.

The even tenor of his rural life was suddenly inter-
rupted by the amazing success of the *Life and Opinions
of Tristram Shandy*, the first two volumes of which were
published in 1760.   Garrick liked it, Bishop Warbur-
ton also, while Horace Walpole declared it was " the
talk of the town ".   So Sterne came up to London,
and soon settled down as a fashionable gentleman with
a penchant for sentimental gallantry.   Naturally " the
town " was by no means unanimous in its verdict.
Richardson denounced the book as execrable, Dr.
Johnson took exception to its indecency, and both
Goldsmith and Smollett ranged themselves among the
hostile critics.

Meanwhile the book, despite denunciation and partly
because of it, enjoyed a wide circulation and, when the
ninth and final volume was published in 1767, Sterne
was quite a public character, on visiting terms with all
the notable men of the day, both literary and political.

But the excitement of this life proved too much for
his delicate health, and he went to the south of France,
after borrowing £20 from Garrick (which he never
repaid).   Needless to say, the gay life of Paris attracted
him and ultimately he settled there for a time with his
wife and daughter.   The fruit of his sojourn abroad
appeared in *A Sentimental Journey* (1768).   If this did

not increase his reputation, it added to his admirers. Horace Walpole, who had been bored by *Tristram*, approved of his new volume.

But the end was near. His health had never been robust and his life abroad did not tend to restore it. Soon after his return to London he died of pleurisy in lodgings at Bond Street (1768), his last words being, " Now it has come ".

What is Sterne's contribution to the development of the English novel ?

Richardson had given sentimentality, Fielding humour, Smollett liveliness. Sterne blends humour and sentiment in a way peculiarly his own and, although structurally he defies every convention of the novel, yet he develops still further the art of characterisation.

Incident is non-existent in Sterne's fiction; there is neither chronology nor progression. His novels are a long parenthesis—a colossal aside to the reader. Yet despite the chaotic incoherence of his method of story-telling, his effects are made with consummate ease.

He is sentimental and humorous, but in a way quite alien to the way of his contemporaries. He makes no attempt, with Richardson, at elaborate analysis; does not vie with Fielding in rolling his jest about with genial mirth, or emulate the uproarious glee of Smollett. Everything is done by the art of insidious suggestion : he never cries, he merely flutters his eyelids; never laughs, merely sniggers. This is due to no consideration of delicacy, for the indecency of Sterne is as flagrant as any of the time, but because he relished leering innuendo.

He arrests attention by what he leaves unsaid. Yet, disagreeable as is his indecency, insufferable as is some of his sentiment, distractedly bewildering as his method may be, of his fine literary craftsmanship there can be no question.

A more careful consideration of his qualities as a writer will reveal this.

Characteristics

(a) *Subtlety of Humour.*—Sterne's involved, rambling style and inconsequential manner owe no little to Rabelais and Robert Burton. Stylists, however, have a way of pilfering pleasantly from one another. Elia himself has many echoes of Sir Thomas Browne; and nearer our own time Stevenson—one of the most delightful of prosemen—frankly owned to being the " sedulous ape " to such men as Hazlitt.

Too much, therefore, must not be made of Sterne's indebtedness to others, since the real question is not what he took from others, but what he added to his borrowings. Sterne certainly repaid his creditors. He had a fine artistic sense, and developed a style that he made his own, by virtue of his peculiar humour, which has little in common with Rabelais' uproarious, full-blooded mirth, or Burton's dry, scholarly wit.

Sterne's indecency is obvious enough—and on the first reading it will seem more insistent than it really is

—it will distract our attention from the exquisite art by which Sterne will delicately construct his characterisation or atmospherically suggest his scenes.   It is here that his humour plays, with the swift illumination of summer lightning, over his subject, delighting the reader, who has learnt to ignore the indecencies of behaviour in favour of the scrupulous decencies of art —which Sterne rarely fails to respect.   To better appreciate the humour, we may turn more especially to the characterisation.

(b) *Subtlety   of   Characterisation.*—That   sensitive, highly self-conscious temperament characteristic of both Richardson and Sterne undoubtedly helped them in niceties of characterisation.   Its drawbacks are that it leads easily into hysterical emotion ; its advantages, that it enables its possessor to distinguish shades of feeling and sensibility overlooked by heartier, stronger-fibred natures.

The visualising power exerts some repression on the prolixity of the writer, and this is all to its advantage ; and the sensibility that is always vacillating between humour and pathos helps its possessor to vitalise his creations.   Sterne's supreme invention is his invention of Uncle Toby.   In some ways Uncle Toby is like Parson Adams : he is eccentric, and has beneath his grotesqueries simplicity, charm, soundness of heart. But if the framework is not dissimilar, the detailed effects by which the character is built up are far subtler. There is a curious intimacy about Sterne's button-holing methods that at times impresses the reader with a greater sense of actuality than he ever feels in turning over the pages of Sterne's contemporaries.

The characterisation is less diverse than in Fielding, less uniformly interesting. But in a few cases it is of the finest quality. None but Sterne could have drawn that delightful kitchen scene at the inn, with the Reverend Mr. Yorick's curate smoking by the fire and suggesting all manner of things by his periods of silence.

In the province of characterisation Sterne has his own particular niche of fame. No one who is interested in this fascinating aspect of fiction can neglect him.

Chapter Eight

Women Novelists (1696—1832)

SEX is not merely a simple matter of physical differentiation, as some imagine it. Indeed, in its ultimate analysis it is a psychical problem; and it is this fact that lends so great an interest to the contributions made by women to literature.

Partly through the exigencies of their historical development, partly because of their psychological characteristics, women have, with certain reservations, proved literary artists of the secondary order only. As poets, philosophers, historians, they have proved on the whole inferior to men; but in the art of fiction they can certainly claim equality, and they can do so not because they rival men on their own special masculine ground, but because, owing to their femininity, they bring into prose certain qualities in which they excel and in which men are as a rule deficient.

Every man has something of the woman in him, every woman something of the man; and this psychical element fluctuates so remarkably that some men are more feminine than masculine, some women more masculine than feminine.

What results from this? From the literary point

of view, we find that where the two elements are proportionately mingled we get the happiest result. Among the men our greatest writers have been those who have had a good share of what we call feminine qualities; among the women, those who have achieved the highest triumphs have been those who with their own feminine gifts have combined a measure also of the masculine.

The masculine qualities comprehend a broad grasp of principles, a logical constructive power, and a faculty for dealing largely and sanely with the big issues of life. The feminine qualities, on the other hand, lie in subtlety rather than vigour of perception, an intuitive insight into the delicate complexities of character, and an intensity and tenacity of passion.

As illustrations of the masculine and feminine methods of approaching the social life of the late eighteenth century we have Fielding and Jane Austen, each of them essentially a painter of manner, concerned in the differences between town and country, satirical in treatment, eschewing sentiment as far as possible. Between them we have a wonderful picture of the time, and the one complements the other; the one bold, dashing, painting in strong, vivid colours; the other delicate, subtle, avoiding violent contrasts, and dealing rather in nuances.

But the feminine note in fiction—the woman's point of view—only gradually found artistic expression, as we shall see if we briefly review the earlier phases of novel-writers.

One of the earliest Englishwomen to write fiction was Mrs. Aphra Behn, who had lived her early life in India, and later on at Antwerp, before she settled in England.

Writing at a time when the old-fashioned romance was in favour and in its worst, its most prolix and tawdriest days, she is noteworthy for the use she made of everyday facts and experience, thus anticipating the method of Defoe. But she has nothing of Defoe's genius for actualising her material, and could not escape the " high-falutin' " style of the elder Romanticism.

But the fact that in *Oroonoko* (1696) she made use of her acquaintance with Eastern races, and that in *The Fair Jilt* she paints a modern adventuress, distinctly Continental in type, is certainly to her credit. Her technique is imperfect and imitative. She has little idea of putting the woman's point of view. Had she done this she would have stood on a far higher level, for she was a woman of intelligence. As it is, she follows in the wake of the male story-teller.

When we come to the early years of the eighteenth century, it is manifest that women are beginning to realise their aptitude for novel-writing.

Immediate successors to Mrs. Behn, and contemporaries of Defoe, were Mrs. Manley, with her *New Atlantis* (1709), and Mrs. Haywood with her Utopian *Memoirs*. These two ladies were prolific writers, and Mrs. Haywood dealt largely with the short story.

Their early work is extremely artificial, and Mrs.

Manley died before the great era of the novel inaugur-
ated by Richardson and Fielding. But some idea of
the influence of these writers can be gained by comparing the earlier work of Mrs. Haywood with her
later novels, written about the mid-century. All of
these show that the imitative faculty is largely in the
ascendant still. Yet the woman writer of the day did
exhibit from time to time traces of that aptitude for
detailed effects, and little subtleties of observation, in
which she was to score so remarkably later on.

Miss Fielding—Henry Fielding's sister—owed more
to Richardson than to the author of *Tom Jones*.
Selecting an environment of adventure ill suited to
her powers, she none the less showed in *David Simple*
(1744) a gift of drawing character greatly in excess of
previous writers. The book was praised by Richardson, who seized this opportunity to disparage her
brother.

Later on we have a certain imaginative power shown
by Frances Sheridan—mother of the dramatist—in
her *Memoirs of Miss Sidney Biddulph* (1761).

Then towards the close of the age come yet greater
signs of promise. Of Mrs. Radcliffe mention is made
in Vol. IV. Her influence on her generation and on
her successors is indubitable, despite her crudeness
and absurdities.

But most of the feminine pioneers in fiction had
seriously handicapped themselves by choosing for
their medium the romantic type of fiction and, despite
Mrs. Radcliffe's success, this is not to their advantage.

Romanticism to be effective demands a broad, massive treatment rather than a subtle, detailed one. It was not in romance that woman was to gain her laurels, but in her own particular realm of experience—at the fireside.

The Robertsonian School of Drama has been dubbed the "Cup-and-Saucer School"; the term is equally applicable to the fiction of Miss Burney and Miss Austen.

What helped women like Fanny Burney and Maria Edgeworth, Susan Ferrier, and above all Jane Austen, to realise the true extent of their power and to give us the fruit of their own experiences of life, rather than imitations of the man's point of view, was the change of manners that took place at the close of the eighteenth century. The coarse brutality of Fielding and Smollett's day gives way to an era when a greater refinement and a quieter taste of life became fashionable. This was clearly advantageous to the woman writer; and four women in particular—three women of considerable talent, one woman of genius—occupy an important place in the development of the English novel.

Hannah More (1745–1833) was the daughter of a Gloucestershire schoolmaster, and the friend of Garrick, by whom she was introduced to the Johnson circle. Her single novel, *Coelebs in Search of a Wife* (1809), shows the satirical bent that was to find such lively expression in the feminine fiction of the near future. But Fanny Burney's *Evelina* is the first book of distinctive literary power in this direction.

Fanny Burney (1752–1840) came of a Norfolk family, being born at King's Lynn, where her father was an organist. Her girlhood was spent in London, and from an early age she showed a passion for writing, greatly to the dismay of her stepmother, who thought such pursuits were unladylike. Impressed, no doubt, by this unfavourable opinion, the sensitive story-teller solemnly burnt her first novel, *The History of Caroline Evelyn*; but stories have a strange vitality of their own which defies material destruction, and it was not long before the history of Caroline became incarnate again in *Evelina, or the History of a Young Lady's Entrance into the World*, published anonymously. The success of the book was instantaneous and the author's name soon leaked out. Fanny Burney found herself famous, approved of by the great, gruff Doctor himself, and warmly praised by such men as Burke and Sir Joshua Reynolds. The book is an admirable picture of the manners of the time, from the woman's point of view. Of humour there is a pleasant spice, though it is subdued; of characterisation there is singularly little; and there is next to no sentiment. In fact, the book lives by its spirited and delicate externalisation of the life of her age. Evelina herself is not interesting; her conventionality and self-effacement make her a colourless young woman; but some of the coarser feminine types are excellently handled, and the pictures of the eighteenth-century " blood ", from the feminine standpoint, is undeniably effective.

The " motif " of the story, that of a young lady of good family and slender fortune, ignorant of the world, trying to make her way in the London life of the time, was perhaps suggested by a novel by Mrs. Frances Brooke, entitled *The Excursion* (1777). Certainly Fanny Burney knew of the novel and was acquainted with the writer, whom she described as possessing an " agreeable ugliness ". Mrs. Brooke's novel is devoid of merit; in treatment and method Miss Burney owed nothing to her friend.

The success of *Evelina* encouraged her to write a successor, and in 1782 *Cecilia, or the Memoirs of an Heiress* was published, a story of family pride, that lacked the freshness of its predecessor. Her last two tales, *Camilla* (1796) and *The Wanderer* (1814), were very feeble productions, largely due to the fact that she attempted to depict sides of life of which she had no experience, and partly also to her departing from the simplicity of her early manner in order to copy the Johnsonian period.

At her best in *Evelina*, her delightful *Diary*, and in parts of *Cecilia*, she showed a delicacy of satire and a faithful observation, above all a genuinely distinctive point of view, assuredly not without their influence on her similar though greater successor—Jane Austen.

Maria Edgeworth, the daughter of a gentleman who owned some property in Co. Longford, Ireland, was born at Black Bourton, near Reading, in 1767, and until the age of fifteen resided in England, eventually migrating to the family estate of Edgeworthstown;

her father, himself a keen educationist, took considerable interest in her training. Literary power early showed itself, and her first work, when she was but fifteen, was a translation of Madame de Genlis' *Adéle et Théodore*, a collection of letters on education; later she was called upon to assist her father in a book on *Practical Education*, his own large family of twenty-one children giving him ample scope for putting his theories to the test. Maria Edgeworth was a prolific writer on educational matters, and published *The Parent's Assistant*, in six volumes, in 1800; but her real power lay in the domain of fiction, and particularly in the delineation of Irish peasant characters. Her first novel was written before she was twenty, though it did not appear till 1814, under the title of *Patronage*. In 1800 the famous *Castle Rackrent* was published, and *Belinda* a year later. She also wrote a large number of tales for the young, some comic dramas published in 1817, and in 1820 the *Memoirs* of her father. She died in 1849.

Maria Edgeworth shows greater vivacity and a more genial breadth than Fanny Burney, but less delicacy of touch, though her educational theories, largely inspired by Thomas Day and by her father, hindered her as a literary artist. " It has been my daughter's aim ", said Richard Lovell Edgeworth, " to promote by all her writings, the progress of education from the cradle to the grave." Unhappily, this is true, yet despite the strenuous didacticism and moral aim of her earlier tales for children, her shrewd sense of character and her liveliness often triumph over the moralist in her. Her Irishmen are real Irishmen, and her success as a writer of Irish life inspired Scott, so he assures us with his characteristic generosity and modesty.

Susan Ferrier (1782–1854) was the daughter of a clerk of the Court of Session, Edinburgh, a colleague of Sir Walter Scott, whose long friendship with her and experience of her tactful sympathy helped to lighten the burden of his later years. Scott was also a great admirer of her work and, while her identity remained undiscovered, he was credited with its production.

An interesting and characteristic fact about Susan Ferrier is that she wrote only three novels : *Marriage* (1818), *The Inheritance* (1824), and *Destiny* (1831), and despite the urgent appeal of her publisher and the unequivocal success of her stories, she declined to add to their number. What Miss Edgeworth did for Irish life, Miss Ferrier did for Scottish. The two writers had no little in common : humour, observation, and a vein of earnest didacticism; but Miss Ferrier's work shows greater variety.

The idea of *Marriage*—the incursion of the fashionable young woman into the rough, dour atmosphere of a Highland home—is carried out with abundant force and humour. Her father, an impecunious peer, nourishes ambitious notions for his daughter's future, and when she elopes with a good looking but poor young Scotsman he promptly disowns her. Accordingly, her husband takes her to his father's house, which Lady Juliana idealises in her own mind as a romantic and delightful place. The reality proves a severe shock.

Another name that belongs to this period, although the writer lived on, like Miss Ferrier, to the mid-nineteenth century, is Miss Mary Russell Mitford (1787–1855). She was a gentle, kindly woman, burdened with a plausible, spendthrift father, of the Horace Skimpole genus, in whom she credulously trusted. Her work is of miscellaneous character; she wrote verse, tried her hand at tragedies, and later in her life wrote a disappointing autobiography.

Despite the fact that she had known many interesting people, she had small gift of making them live in the pages of her *Recollections* (1852), though their range is surprising, including on the one hand references to the prodigality of Sheridan's entertainment, and on the other pleasant references to James Payne and Ruskin.

But the work by which she will be known is *Our Village* (1824–32), a series of charming sketches of rural life, flavoured with delicate humour, and unmistakably feminine throughout. Living through the revival of Romanticism, she belongs by temperament and method to the later eighteenth century, to the school of manners of which Fanny Burney was the pioneer and Jane Austen the mistress craftswoman.

Jane Austen was born on December 16, 1775, at Steventon, near Basingstoke, a tiny village amid the chalk hills of North Hants. Her father was rector of the place, her mother, Cassandra, the daughter of the Rev. Thomas Leigh, and niece of the famous wit, Theophilus Leigh, for many years Master of Balliol. Jane was the youngest of seven children, and her life was singularly tranquil and uneventful. Occasional private theatricals, and a rare visit to Bath and London, broke the gentle monotony of her home life. We gather that she was a great reader, knew something of modern languages, and was an excellent needlewoman, " especially in satin stitch ". Little, however, is known of her, and none of the letters that survive tells us anything of her inner life.

In person she was " a tall, slender, clear brunette ", with hazel eyes, good features, and curly brown hair. In temperament cool, detached, reserved, keenly humorous. Beyond the mild flirtations of the countryside that accompanied dancing and tea-making and theatricals, we have no evidence of any emotional crisis in her life. In fact, at almost every point she presents the antithesis to the other daughter of a country parson destined later on to make the Yorkshire moors articulate. She died in 1817, of consumption, and was buried at Winchester in the north aisle of the cathedral.

Jane Austen was a born story-teller; she wrote from sheer love of writing, her stories being published anonymously in her lifetime.

Someone has said that in politics she was a mild Tory. Mildness and equability certainly characterised

her general attitude throughout life.   There were no
extremes in her nature.   Singularly judicial, she formed
no violent estimates of people, and is scrupulously fair
in her pictures.

About what are her pictures ?

The tattle, the trivialities of life in a small country
town, when tea-time was an exciting event and a
subscription ball a crisis in one's career; when romance
expressed itself in country walks (usually with a
chaperone), when the tragedy hinged upon the non-
appearance at the cross-roads of the agreeable young
man who danced so well at the ball.

Faithful observation, personal detachment, and a
fine sense of ironic comedy are among Jane Austen's
chief characteristics as a writer.   As a testimony to
her excellent sense and good feeling, one may say
that, subjected to all the snobberies that abound in
provincial towns, she never showed any trace of being
affected by them.   Not greatly affected by social
miseries, she was in a measure sympathetic and tolerant
towards the poor; and without the faintest weakness
for the aristocrat and well-to-do.   She did not pretend
to be a social reformer and it is useless and foolish to
gird at her because the underworld is always kept out
of view.   But this one may always find in her books—
an entire absence of simulation of feeling.   Folly
she ridicules wherever she finds it.   Sin she excuses
wherever she can, judging a man and a woman by
their opportunities in life.

Five novels alone stand to her credit :   *Pride and*

Prejudice, 1796–97; *Northanger Abbey*, 1798; *Sense and Sensibility*, 1797; *Mansfield Park*, 1814; *Emma*, 1816. *Persuasion*, written in 1816, was not published till after her death; another novel, *Lady Susan*, was never published, and *The Watsons* she left unfinished.

No one has expressed the peculiar quality of her art more happily than Scott : " The big bow-wow strain I can do myself, like any now going ; but the exquisite touch that renders commonplace things and characters interesting from the truth of the description and the sentiment is denied me."

The secret of her power lies in the complete mastery she has as an artist over her material. She was finely alive to her limitations, never touched a character or scene she did not know, and never invented a story or personage which she did not subject to such minutely intimate treatment that the reader feels that it is all a fragment of autobiography.

Characteristics

(a) *Her Faithful Observation.*—The art of observation is the art which every novelist necessarily excels in, for the first essential in any story is the illusion of reality. No exuberance or fertility of imagination can take its place ; nor is this illusion possible without the patient, observant fidelity of the painter with the phenomena of life as they present themselves to the painter's vision.

Defoe was a sound observer ; he knew his middle-class citizens and he knew his vagabonds, but the examples he gives us are types rather than individuals. Crusoe is a God-fearing London citizen ready to combine good sense and piety; Moll Flanders, a ne'er-do-well; Captain Singleton, a dashing adventurer. We appreciate the class to which they belong and their fidelity to life. But they are not individualised. Richardson, far more concerned with individualisation, gives greater solidarity to his characters—his feminine ones especially; but, being devoid of humour, his power to visualise, though strong, is not varied. It has been said that we can see all round his characters. Certain qualities he sees very clearly, but one and all are too drenched in sentiment for any complete appraisement. Fielding's great humour intensifies his vision, and in such characters as Parson Adams and Squire Western we feel in the presence of individual characters, not types.

The special charm in Jane Austen's novels lies, not in any deep insight into character, but in the fine impartiality with which she individualises and differentiates them. Her compass is not wide, but within it she never fails. It is certainly significant that her favourite poet should have been Crabbe, for Crabbe was a minute observer. He described Nature like an imaginative naturalist, and much as he loved the country poor he never spares them, never idealises them. His pictures are finely dispassionate. Jane Austen also loved her kind—loved them with the joy of the scientist. She found them crowding about her tea-parties, her church gatherings, her balls, and she reproduces them for us with an unemotional fidelity sometimes a little cruel, but never unfair.

She was perfectly acquainted with her *métier*, and never attempted what was out of her line.   Once, on being asked to write an historical romance, she replied :

> " I am fully sensible that (such a romance) might be much more to the purpose of profit or popularity than such pictures of domestic life in country villages as I deal in.   But I could no more write a romance than an epic poem.   I could not sit seriously down to write a serious romance under any other motive than to save my life ; and if it were indispensable for me to keep it up and never relax into laughing at myself or at any other people, I am sure I should be hung before I had finished the first chapter.   No, I must keep to my own style and go on in my own way ; and though I may never succeed again in that, I am convinced I should totally fail in any other."

Nor did she concern herself with social problems, and we feel no more the curse of poverty in her books than we feel the power of passion that sweeps through the writings of Charlotte and Emily Brontë.

It is notable that, for all her minute observation, she rarely describes personal appearance.   Jane Eyre and Becky Sharp are familiar enough in their outward appearance ; but Elizabeth Bennet and Miss Bates we could recognise only when we had heard them talk.

Humour touches and illuminates all her best characters.

Mrs. Bennet laments that after her husband's death she may be turned out.   " My dear," says her husband, " do not give way to such gloomy thoughts. Let us hope for better things. Let us flatter ourselves that I may be the survivor."

(b) *Her Power of Self-detachment.*—She was serene and equable, caring for many things but nothing in an especial degree. Most things amused her; few things angered her. She greets those she dislikes with a slight, contemptuous smile; she never rages at them, as Fielding would. And this power of self-detachment, of eliminating from her story those strong predilections that often sway an author's creations, enabled her to be an artist pure and simple. There is no didacticism, no philosophy, no propaganda in her fiction. We have a perfect picture of provincial life in the early eighteenth century; a delicate water-colour to put beside the more vigorous oil-painting of Fielding.

(c) *Her sense of Comedy.*—Miss Austen's tales are not laughter provoking, but they leave behind them a rippling sense of pleasure. Her humour is quiet, delicate, ironical. She is not a satirist, for satire connotes moral purpose. Jane Austen never lashes our follies, she slightly arches her eyebrows and passes on. She touches the humorous side of almost every scene she sees or imagines, whether the fear of ghosts (*Northanger Abbey*), private theatricals (*Mansfield Park*), a picnic (*Emma*), a proposal (*Persuasion*). But she never exaggerates the fun.

At a time when sentimentalism was in the hey-day of its glory, when folk wept over Richardson and shuddered over Mrs. Radcliffe, or, if indisposed for these things, relished the stronger fare of Fielding and Smollett, the departure made by Jane Austen required no small courage and self-reliance. She was the disciple of no school, though well read and appreciative of the great writers of the day. She felt she could do certain things well, and she did them, neither deterred by lack of appreciation nor tempted to seek popularity by reason of material disadvantages.

Her circumstances helped her to give that finish and delicacy to her work that, had Fate been harsher, might have proved impossible. There was a cool radiance about all her work, a happy sanity. It was part of her everyday life, to be placed aside should a visitor come, to be resumed when he left; to be pursued unostentatiously and tranquilly in the midst of the family circle. She knew precisely what she wanted to do, and she did it in the way that suited her best. Certainly she has had her reward.

Chapter Nine

Minor Prose

MEMOIR literature enjoys a greater vogue in France than in England, but the zest for experimentalising in literature that began to be noticeable about the close of the seventeenth century and continued throughout the eighteenth led to the creation of a class of books written for amusement rather than for any ulterior purpose. Authorship became a pleasant game for many people of leisure, and those who in an earlier age would have indited sonnets and penned amatory lyrics now turned their attention to satiric verse, gossipy letters on things in general, or political squibs.

By means of this light, discursive literature we have a steady flow of illuminating gossip on the life of the time, highly valuable to the social historian.

Lady Mary Wortley Montagu came of an aristocratic Whig family, was connected by blood with the diarist Evelyn, and was also a distant relation of Pepys. This link with the great diarists agreeably symbolises the literary affinity that binds together the diarist and the memoir writers.

Born in 1689, she was very beautiful as a child and her proud father is said to have toasted her at the famous Kit Cat Club. His ideas on the subject of marriage, however, did not coincide with hers, so in 1712 she eloped with Edward Wortley Montagu, who was greatly attracted by her graces of mind and body. In 1716 Montagu went as ambassador to Constantinople, accompanied by his wife, and in this way material was collected for her *Turkish Letters*. Many of these had been prepared with a view to publication but, though known to a circle of friends, were not published until after Lady Mary's death. The writer had donned Turkish dress while abroad and made a close study of Turkish customs. This enabled her to dispel a good deal of prejudice and ignorance about the Ottoman character. On her return she lived in England for some years and then, unaccompanied by her husband, went abroad again for a considerable period, soon after her daughter, in true filial imitation, had eloped with Lord Bute. From Italy she wrote frequently to her daughter, and the letters are among her best. In them her keen humour and intellectual alertness are clearly shown; she is equally happy either in describing her life at home (not far from Brescia) or commenting on the fiction of Richardson and Smollett, which had been imported for her special benefit. In 1761 she returned to England, only to die in the next year.

As a writer her fame rests entirely on her letters. She wrote satirical verse in imitation of Gay and Pope, the lighter verse tolerably good, the more serious indifferently so. Her *Diary*, which might have proved of the greatest interest, was left to her daughter and burnt by her just before her death.

Although there was no open rupture with her husband, her deliberate seclusion in Italy for so many years gave rise to many rumours and scandals, and among her enemies were Pope and Walpole.

Undoubtedly she was the cleverest woman of her day, with a certain hardness in her nature and with no wealth of wit sufficient to compensate for this; but with much solid sense and keen insight into character. As a letter-writer she has a clear, lively, and natural style.

Another letter-writer and diarist is Mary Clavering, who married Lord Cowper. She entered the household of Queen Caroline in 1714, and kept a diary which, though much of it was destroyed by fire, gives amusing sidelights on the doings of the Hanoverian Court. It has no special literary charm, but is certainly interesting in its way. Lady Cowper knew most of the literary men of the time—Swift, Young, Gay, Arbuthnot, Horace Walpole, Lord Chesterfield— and was on excellent terms with Pope.

Another contemporary is John, Lord Hervey, of whom Lady Mary Montagu said, " The human race was divided into men, women, and Herveys ". He was an excellent wit and a rhymester of fair capacity, and between his family and Lady Mary there was a strong bond of friendship.

Naturally, therefore, Pope disliked him and pilloried him in the *Dunciad*. Nor was Pope his only mordant critic. However, he could take care of him-

self and retaliated with equal spirit and bitterness in
his *Memoirs*.

Sir Robert Walpole made use of Hervey's acid
pen while in power. Hervey took service under the
Government as Lord Privy Seal, distinguishing himself as a vigorous pamphleteer. His *Memoirs*, published after his death, give a highly satirical picture of
Court life during the reign of George II and, with the
exception of the Queen and the Princess Caroline,
none escaped his gift of cynical portraiture.

Of a very different stamp is Philip Dormer Stanhope,
fourth Earl of Chesterfield, born in 1694. After a
brief but fairly important political career (at one
time he was Viceroy of Ireland), he retired upon
literature in 1748, whether from deafness or *ennui*, or a
combination of these, it is hard to determine. His
literary fame rests upon his letters to his illegitimate
son. As a letter-writer he is certainly remarkable,
though in no way like any of the other letter-writers
with whom we have been dealing. Mannered and
circumspect to an irritating degree, he was a good writer
of the precise school, a versatile scholar, and a man of
shrewd judgment.

As for his general outlook on life, perhaps no saying
of his is more self-illuminating than his well-known
dictum : " If there were no God it would be necessary
to create one."

Among the many letter-writers of the time, there is
no one whose personality and work is more original
and provocative than Horace Walpole's.

Horace Walpole, the fourth son of the famous Sir Robert, was born in 1717, went to Eton and Cambridge, and spent his earlier years in travel. Although at a later time he became an active politician, he did not distinguish himself in this capacity, and his fame rests on his varied contributions to literature.

Among his more notable writings are *Historic Doubts*, *Anecdotes of Paintings*, *The Castle of Otranto*, and, above all, his letters.

Of his *Castle of Otranto* some detailed mention is made in Volume IV. Here he may be regarded merely as a letter-writer. With the exception of Pope, it is questionable whether any writer of the age caught more exquisitely the affectations and artificialities of the time than did this fop of genius.

He is the very first prince of gossips, and the acrid effeminacy of the man, little as it redounds to his credit as a personality, proved invaluable to him in this capacity. Had he been less fond of tea-parties, less prone to tattle, his letters would have lost half their savour. Beside him Lady Mary and Lord Chesterfield seem astoundingly heavy-handed in their satire. Horace Walpole had a delicacy of touch, a neat and airy deftness, more Gallic than English.

That this cynical trifler should be one of the precursors of the Romantic revival, one of the pioneers of the medieval enthusiasts, is among the pleasant paradoxes of literary history.

Perhaps the cynical and flippant side of the man has been over-emphasised. We have to remember the tone and character of the society in which he moved, and when in his letters we come across glimpses of genuine friendliness and kindness of heart, and recall his fine enthusiasm for our old cathedrals and his undoubted artistic feeling and predilection for the mystery and romance of a bygone age, we may not unreasonably conjecture that a good deal of his trifling was a pose and that there was more substance in him than is commonly allowed.

However that may be, and taking him at his own estimate in his letters, he is certainly a consummate maker of trifles and an admirable painter of the foibles of his time.

Chapter Ten

History and Scholarship (16th to 18th Centuries)

(i) From Bacon to Robertson

THE art of the historian and the art of the novelist are closely related. In both cases a faculty for story-telling and a sense of characterisation are of high importance. There is a scientific side to history, with which fiction is not concerned, demanding such gifts as balance of judgment, veracity of outlook, and power of reasoning. History is not a science, and by the variability of its data cannot be regarded as such, but a scientific study of its phenomena is certainly helpful in giving it weight and value. It is clear that, as students of literature, we are not concerned here with the scientific side. What does concern us is the artistic side—the power of painting human life and human institutions with vitality and actuality. That the picture may be one-sided, perchance based on documents of doubtful value, will prejudice its scientific value, but need not divest it of fidelity to human nature and arresting power over the imagination. So while veracity and balance of judgment are rightly considered as essential to the great historian, he must first of all be a literary artist in some measure, or his other qualities will count as nothing.

The first important departure from the crowd of chroniclers and annalists which meets us in the Middle Ages and Earlier Renascence is signalised by Bacon in his *History of the Reign of Henry VII*. Here, at any rate, there is something of the art and insight without which the historian becomes little better than a compiler. There is a measure of the same seriousness of purpose in Lord Herbert of Cherbury's *Life of Henry VIII*, and Lord Herbert was better circumstanced than Bacon when he wrote his history in being able to avail himself of many documents.

There is sanity and sobriety in Archbishop Spottiswoode's *History of the Church of Scotland*, while in Irish history Spenser's *View of the Present State of Ireland*, dominated as it is by matters of personal interest, is none the less a remarkable picture of Elizabethan politics.

At this point something may be said of some of the materials of history in which the Stuart period is rich. Strictly speaking, State papers and letters do not belong to historical literature, except where here and there a letter or document may possess some artistic value apart from the bald statement of fact contained in it. But the stuff of history bears so intimate a connection with historical literature, and often merges so insensibly into it, that it is scarcely out of place to devote some attention to the matter.

John Rushworth's collection of *Private Passages of*

State and *Remarkable Proceedings in Five Parliaments* is the first really important collection of English State Papers. Rushworth was Clerk's Assistant to the House of Commons, and secretary to the Council of War in 1645. These volumes contain valuable first-hand evidence of the political and ecclesiastical embroilments of the time. The last volume ends with the trial of Strafford.

Thurloe's well-known name comes next—John Thurloe, the secretary of Oliver Cromwell—and in his collection of State Papers he deals with much that throws light on the policy of Cromwell, both at home and abroad. These may be supplemented by the letters and speeches of Cromwell himself, made familiar to us by Carlyle. He was a born letter-writer, and his rugged forcefulness, his religious conviction, and shrewd insight, are well exhibited in them.

Equally admirable in a different way is the correspondence of Sir Harry Wotton, the friend of Donne, the author of a fine poem, *Ye meaner Beauties of the Night*, and the subject of an elegy by Cowley and a biography by Izaak Walton.

Born in 1568 in Kent, he was educated at Winchester and Oxford, afterwards spending several years in travel. Under James he was thrice Ambassador at Venice, and finally became Provost at Eton, dying in 1639. He was a voluminous letter-writer, and in his official letters to James he salted his political reports with attractive humour. Outside his correspondence, his literary projects were fragmentary but suggestive, especially the *Characters* of Essex and Buckingham. A pleasant style and a fresh and vigorous outlook distinguish his work. Equally vigorous are the letters of the ill-fated Strafford (1611–40).

Turning to the time of the Civil War, we have, in addition to the material furnished by Thurloe and Cromwell, the Fairfax *Correspondence* and the *Letters and Papers* of the Verney family down to 1639, merging later into the *Memoirs of the Verney Family*.

A good picture is given in the Verney *Memoirs* of the discomforts and miseries suffered by the families of Royalists during the Civil War. The discomforts, one might say, were general—London was in a perpetual ferment and unrest from the day when Charles attempted the arrest of five Members.

Finally, we come to the *Familiar Letters* of James Howell, Historiographer Royal to Charles II. These are more in the nature of political table-talk and brief essays. He was a strong anti-Puritan, and was not unduly particular as to accuracy of statement, but he was often clear, pithy, and humorous; even when discursive and gossipy, he rarely fails to be interesting.

Clarendon, in his *History of the Great Rebellion* (published 1702–4), carries us a stage farther in the development of historical literature. If as stylist he is inferior in clarity and grace to some who preceded him, he has a greater gift of narrative and a remarkable faculty for visualising his characters. In his sketches of Falkland, of Godolphin, and Chillingworth, he has given us live and memorable portraits.

Contemporary with these writers is Gilbert Burnet (1643–1715), whose *History of the Reformation* (1679, 1682, and the third volume in 1714) had many of the qualities that distinguished Clarendon's work. It is, of course, frankly polemical and Protestant. There is an arresting quality in Burnet's ecclesiastical history, that marks also his later *History of My Own Times* (1723). More agreeable and varied as a writer than Clarendon, he is inferior to him in his faculty for telling a story. But there is life in his narrative, and actuality. Partisanship marks all the writers of this time but both in Clarendon and Burnet, with all their limitations, there is an undeniable sense of reality which is a valuable acquisition to the art of history-making.

Strype (1643–1737), equally well known for his *Ecclesiastical Memorials* (1721), has little of the literary power of Burnet and Clarendon, but he was a painstaking and sincere writer who took his work with a high seriousness that showed the increasing interest in scholarly historical research.

Following these writers came Jeremy Collier, with his thoughtful, erudite, and somewhat pedestrian *Ecclesiastical History* (1708–14), and Daniel Neal, whose vigorous *History of the Puritans* (1732) is a valuable contribution to the history of Nonconformity.

Scotland has reason to be proud of Andrew Fletcher (1655–1716) of Saltoun, a scholar and traveller, who had been trained early in life by Burnet himself, and whose writings on contemporary political subjects are marked by political insight and a charm and liveliness of style uncommon at this time among Scottish prose-writers. In one of his shorter pieces on government there is to be found that well-known saying referred to " a very wise man ", that " if a man were permitted to make all the ballads, he need not care who should make the laws of the nation ".

Henry St. John, 1st Viscount Bolingbroke, was born of ancient lineage, at Battersea, in 1678, and educated at Eton. Profligate and dissipated in youth, he afterwards became one of the most brilliant and versatile men of his day—and the " guide, philosopher, and friend " of Pope.

His chief works are *Reflections upon Exile*, written during his first period in France; *Letters on the Study of History*, and a *Letter on the True Use of Retirement*, during his second visit; *Letters on the Spirit of Patriotism*; and *Idea of a Patriot King*. His death took place in 1751.

Bolingbroke's literary style is strongly impressed by his power as an orator. The insincerity of the man and the superficiality of his methods must not blind us to the clarity, the neatness, the easy wit of his style. As a master of political invective he has few superiors; he was a good letter-writer, and it has been said that he was " the first English writer to recognise and illustrate the cardinal principle of the continuity of history ".

Roger North's (1653–1734) *Lives of the Norths*

(1742–44) illustrates the growing interest in characterisation befitting an age of fiction. It is rich in literary grace and in that lucidity of method and shrewdness of outlook characteristic of the best writers of the time.

About the middle of the eighteenth century the art of history-making shows still further development in the hands of Hume, Robertson, and Gibbon.

The clear, ironical method of Hume lends especial value to his fragmentary *History of England*, over the writing of which he took eight years. If less remarkable as an historian than as a philosopher, there is no doubt that his intellectual power and philosophical acuteness proved valuable assets in his historical writings.

William Robertson (1721–1793), with less intellectual force but no less literary ability, discloses in his *History of Scotland* and his *History of the Reign of the Emperor Charles V* (1769) careful research and philosophical breadth. Perhaps the point of superiority in these over earlier writers is the growth of the judicial and critical spirit and the broader philosophic outlook.

Goldsmith, by virtue of his delightful style, and Smollett, with his vigorous gift of narrative, are names worth remembering in historical work, but they did nothing for the development of this subject, and can scarcely be called historians. What they did was to popularise history and cause it to bulk more prominently in the public view.

(ii) Edward Gibbon

We now come to Edward Gibbon, born at Putney in 1737. He was a delicate, precocious boy, educated at Westminster School and Magdalen College, Oxford, whither he went in 1752 " with a stock of erudition that might have puzzled a doctor, and a degree of ignorance of which a schoolboy would have been ashamed ".

During the five years he was abroad he travelled considerably, and while in Rome conceived the idea of writing his *History of the Decline and Fall of the Roman Empire*, and for six years was at work on the first volume, published in 1776.

With late years came sorrow, bereavements, and indifferent health, and death came suddenly on January 16, 1794.

Gibbon was by far the greatest historian of his age. As a literary stylist he is sufficiently remarkable, with his clear, imposing, rhythmic prose, but he is even more remarkable for that intuitive faculty that endows some men so richly with the historical sense, quite apart from their scholarship. This faculty it is which enabled Gibbon to present his work as an organic whole, with the details properly subordinate to the main structure.

Perhaps his only serious defect as an historian was his inability to understand enthusiasm and the forces to which enthusiasm could give rise. This was a defect in many writers of his age and, if it qualifies our admiration for him as a thinker, it does not gravely affect his skill as an historian. It is particularly noticeable in his criticism of organised religion. Christianity in especial, with its record of martyrdom or heroic selflessness, was beyond his understanding and sympathy. For this reason his famous fifteenth and sixteenth chapters were found extremely offensive.

That Gibbon was not so scrupulous in examination of his sources as has formerly been supposed, that he is now in many points out of date, that his own want of conviction about some of the most serious problems of life is apparent in his work—these are defects which may be readily admitted. On the positive side, it must also be admitted that his history is peerless in design and structure.

In narrative power, which appears also in his *Memoirs* (1796), the *Letters* (published 1896), and his *Journal* (published 1929), he achieved an elaboration puzzling to the critics of his own day and a masterpiece for any day. The prose which conveys it is rhythmical in a way unique in him and but poorly imitated by followers. Periphrasis is a favourite ornament; the structure of his paragraphs is subtly directed to focus on one point, however great the panorama around it; his sentences are filled with a rhythm which gives them a remarkable swell and surge and ends with notes which echo back over the lines. Any description of his prose necessarily gives the impression that his writing was monotonous. Yet variety is one of

Gibbon's merits—a virtue which rapidly disappears from the prose of an imitator.

Gibbon's prose is not the rhetoric of Burke. It is the prose which can be built up in an age of talkers, for it is an ordering of the rhythms of daily speech. Perhaps it is this quality which gives it blandness, a quiet assurance, something of its carefully contrived variety. Analysis of it is extremely difficult, but one believes that it should proceed in that direction. Is it too much to say that Gibbon re-arranged and pointed daily speech as carefully as Milton constructed his orchestral Blank Verse ? Quotation would take too much space, but what is here meant may be seen in this fragment of a sentence (and the subtlety of the final clause holds part of the secret), in which he says that he was unable to " reflect without pleasure on the bounty of Nature, which cast my birth in a free and civilised country, in an age of science and philosophy, in a family of honourable rank, and decently endowed with the gifts of fortune ".

(iii) Edmund Burke

Edmund Burke, like Gibbon, was one of the great prosemen of the age. Beyond that the two men have nothing in common except being contemporaries and in the same literary set.

May we not imagine that many a young student entering Trinity College, Dublin, has been fired with enthusiasm to emulate one of those two famous Irishmen whose monuments stand like sentinels, on either side, guarding its main entrance—the one Oliver Goldsmith, the other that great orator, statesman, and political writer, Edmund Burke ?

Born in Dublin in 1729, Burke was the son of an Irish lawyer, and educated with two brothers at a Quaker school at Ballitore, Co. Kildare. His father wished him to become a lawyer but the idea displeased the son. Though he came to London and was entered in the Middle Temple, he soon found more congenial company within that famous circle over which Samuel Johnson presided, and concentrated his mind on the study of history and philosophy; the outcome of this was the anonymous publication of *A Vindication of Natural Society* in 1756, and an *Essay on the Sublime and Beautiful*, which attracted so much attention that it was translated into French and German. The following year appeared *A Sketch of American History*, in two volumes; and for several years he wrote the whole of the *Annual Register*, published by Dodsley.

It is not, however, in the domain of literature that Edmund Burke is best known. In 1761 politics claimed him. Acting as private secretary to " Single-speech " Hamilton, the Chief Secretary for Ireland, and four years later to the Marquis of Rockingham, the Prime Minister, paved the way for his entry into Parliament. He was chosen in 1765 as member for Wendover and for twenty-eight years there was scarcely a more prominent figure in the life of St. Stephen's. Certain disturbances rising out of the expulsion of John Wilkes by the House of Commons in 1768 had previous to this inspired his well-known *Thoughts on the Present Discontents* (1770).

Burke reached the pinnacle of fame in 1788, when he led the impeachment of Warren Hastings in a speech which occupied four days, during which he brought before his hearers the most vivid pictures of the beauties of the East as well as the horrors and desolation of the tortured Hindoos. Catholic emancipation, the abolition of the slave trade, and the great French Revolution likewise claimed his attention.

In 1794, retiring from public life to his beautiful home at Beaconsfield, Bucks, he met with a terrible blow in the death of his only son by rapid consumption. Burke's health gradually failed, and he died on July 7, 1797 and was buried in Beaconsfield Church.

Burke is first and foremost an orator. That must be remembered in estimating his manner and matter. He is therefore a great rhetorician, rich in passionate declamation, and excelling where splendour and force are required, though with little power of variety or delicacy of emphasis.

His gifts as a writer are nowhere better displayed than in his magnificent, one-sided *Reflections on the Revolution in France*.

In comparing Burke's prose, at the close of the century, with the prose of Dryden, in its early years, we cannot help noticing the gradual swing back of the pendulum to Renascence models. Flinging off in Dryden all the glitter and colour of the Elizabethan prosemen, striving above all after plainness of speech, homeliness of phrase, and flexibility of method, the prosemen, having tidied up the gorgeous confusion that beset so much of the prose at their start, grew tired of the plain veracity of speech and gradually recaptured some of the golden qualities of the Elizabethan and Caroline writers.

But we are concerned here especially with the literary man as historian. What of Burke in this connection ?

Burke deals with the history of his own time rather than with the past, and his claim upon us as an historian is that he brings to his work a lofty imagination, an impassioned manner, and a philosophical insight—qualities assuredly needed in the making of history. However, they may need balancing by the more pedestrian faculties of precision and judgment.

It is a fine tribute to Burke's power that his work, concerned as it is with the politics of his own age, should possess so much permanent value for the student of literature and history. The subjects with which he is concerned are big and important ones, for the transitional age in which he lived abounded in problems of striking and memorable importance; but his importance is due less to the greatness of his subjects than to the grandeur of his way of approaching them. Today we may realise clearly enough the inevitable character of that " red, fool fury of the Seine ", which Tennyson epitomised in a neat but shallow phrase. But the price paid for the great upheaval, necessary as it may have been, was terrible and lamentable enough; and no one saw this side of it better than Burke, as his glowing tribute to Marie Antoinette testifies.

Sometimes he touches what seems to be a passing phase of political disturbance, as when he deals with the troubles in connection with John Wilkes, but he wrung from these a wise and coolly reasoned discussion of the dangers to English liberty which may lurk even in Parliamentary government. The breadth and largeness of his outlook are nowhere better illustrated than in his speech on *Conciliation with America* (1775), where he makes light of the legal argument in favour of taxing the colonies, taking up his position on the more durable ground of sense and expediency.

There is always with Burke the immediate particular problem, that leads him to some wise and weighty generalisation, which has enriched our store of political maxims long after the occasion that evolved it has been forgotten.

(iv) Scholarly Research

The seventeenth century reaped the advantages of the enthusiastic study of the Classics, made in the heyday of the Renascence. The writers of the sixteenth century had saturated themselves with the master writers of Greece and Rome; it remained for the succeeding age to apply the knowledge thus gained both to the pursuit of science and to literary productiveness. The gain to science we are dealing with elsewhere. The effect upon literature has already concerned us in dealing with the poetry, prose, and drama of the time. Here the more purely academic side will be noted.

Latin was the language favoured in the seventeenth century, as in earlier times, by scholars, though many books were published both in Latin and English. Bacon's *Novum Organum*, and the later disputations of the learned Casaubon with James I, may be instanced as illustrations of this tendency, while it must be remembered that the scientific discoveries of such men as Harvey and Newton were given to the world in Latin. Latin, indeed, was the international medium of communication between men of learning.

The increasing interest in Biblical research, resulting from the Reformation, gave an added stimulus to the study of Greek and Hebrew.

The difference between the scholarly spirit of the sixteenth and that of the seventeenth centuries lay in the sharpened sense of practicality. These languages were used now not merely to indulge the literary temperament, but to further the practical needs of the time. For instance, the earlier study of Classical Antiquities and Ancient Institutions pointed a way for the treatment of English Institutions, and at the universities the investigation of past literatures was guided very largely by the theological bias of the day. To such an extent was this carried that one college authority counselled the study of " Protestant mathematical books ". The enormous concentration of interest on the Bible necessarily weakened scholastic interest in the Greek writers, whose paganism was looked upon as a serious qualification of their authority.

While most of the important scholars devoted themselves to theological matters, rather than to classical studies, while Pearson was expounding the Creed, and William Lloyd, Bishop of St. Asaph, was discoursing on Church History, a great scholar arose, Richard Bentley, whose interests were far wider than we find in those writers.

Born in 1662, he was educated at Wakefield and Cambridge, becoming later a tutor in the house of Benjamin Stillingfleet. Afterwards he became Master of Trinity, gained fame in sedulous controversy as to the rival merits of Ancient and Modern, and died in 1742, leaving behind him a reputation as a gruff north-countryman of vast learning and immense dialectical power.

Unhappily his great and deserved reputation as a scholar was not sufficient for him. Infirmities of temper and a growing arrogance disclosed themselves aggressively in later life, and he showed grievous lack of judgment in essaying the editing of Milton's writings—a task that shows only too clearly his limitations as a man of letters. Before his death Pope had pilloried him, in the *Dunciad*, as a terrible dullard. Dull he may have been and often was in matters of literary taste, but to picture him as merely a high and dry pedant is as absurd as it is unfair.

During the late seventeenth century a vigorous movement was made in the direction of local antiquities, and a number of writers, of great industry, made a notable departure from the old haphazard way of using existing compilations without discrimination, and with method and precision endeavoured to get at their subject by a study of local documents and records and careful topographical investigation. Oxford was the centre of this antiquarian movement, and among the memorable names are Sir William Dugdale, with his *Antiquities of Warwickshire*, Anthony Wood, a diarist and author of *Survey of the Antiquities of Oxford*, Thomas Hearne, Assistant Keeper in the Bodleian Library, whose series of *Mediæval English Church Chronicles* carried the History of England down to the reign of Richard I; and Thomas Tanner, with his account of monastic records, in which he defended the monasteries against the more audacious of the charges brought against them by Protestant historians.

Less solid in learning than these writers, though more attractive as a writer, was John Aubrey, whose *Brief Lives* of famous people were written to help Wood. Aubrey belonged to the pleasant, gossiping order of writer; he was a man of literary fragments, with insufficient perseverance for any solid work on his own account. But he had an excellent eye for foibles of character, as these " lives " testify. He was a born portrait-painter and, unlike many of his age, could be intimate and vivid without being spiteful.

Chapter Eleven

Scots Verse and Prose (1500–1775)

THE vigorous early growth of Scots verse, that followed the death of Chaucer and gave a greater vitality to Scottish literature than to English in the intermediate period preceding the English Renascence, was not maintained. While English poetry was reviving under Wyatt and Surrey and Gascoigne, Scotland did little except grow a crop of satirical verse nourished more or less by the Reformation, with a rough, not wholly unattractive, tang to it but of poor artistic quality. Following this there are two names of some note, contemporary with Sidney and Spenser— Alexander Scott and Alexander Montgomerie.

Of Scott as a man we know little. He seems to have been unhappy both in domestic relations and in his endeavours to make a competency. His work is heterogeneous. Pious and satirical verses jostle with amorous ditties in a manner characteristic of his time. Probably his love-ditties show him in his most attractive manner; these are pleasantly written, showing sincerity and feeling.

Scott's contemporary, Alexander Montgomerie (1555–1610), strikes a stronger and more personal note. He was known as Captain Montgomerie, and served at one time the Regent Morton. His most considerable work is *The Cherrie and the Slae* (Sloe), an allegory, presumably, dealing with the merits of the sweet fruit, that grows high out of reach, and the sloe, small and insignificant beneath it. Familiar abstractions appear : Hope, Reason, Experience, etc., with a running commentary of their own. There are some agreeable passages of description and a few flashes of humour, and the whole poem is written in a curious metre which became popular and evoked many imitations.

Besides this poem, Montgomerie wrote nearly a hundred sonnets, respectable in quality, but not equal to the best work of the Elizabethan sonneteers ; some devotional pieces, and some ribald matter; a burlesque, *Navigation*, and a few love-ditties. His work, on the whole, was more varied and more distinctive than Scott's.

Sir Robert Ayton (1570–1638), born in Fife, was knighted by James I, and played a prominent part in the Court politics of the time. He was a scholar and wrote in many languages, and it is noteworthy that there is no trace of Scots dialect in his English poetry, which shows a sharp cleavage with the elder Scots school of verse.

This cleavage is even more marked in the Earl of Stirling (*c.* 1580–1640), whose lyric work, the " Aurora " collection, is strictly in line with the Elizabethan songwriters, so far as treatment is concerned, though inferior to the best of these. He wrote also tragedies :

Crœsus, Darius, Alexander, Julius Cæsar, dignified and meritorious in many ways, and the *Exhortation to Prince Henry*, somewhat in the vein of Drayton, and held by some to be his best work.

In quality, however, he is easily surpassed by his friend, Drummond of Hawthornden (1585–1649). He was cultured and accomplished; his sonnets, lyrics, elegies, characteristically Jacobean in the school of Donne, display many beauties and felicities.

Doth then the world go thus, doth all thus move ?
Is this the justice which on earth we find ?
Is this that firm decree which all doth bind ?
Are these your influences, Power above ?
These souls which vice's moody mists most blind,
Blind Fortune, blindly, most their friend doth prove;
And they who thee, poor idol Virtue ! love,
Fly like a feather toss'd by storm and wind.
Ah ! if a Providence doth sway this all,
Why should best minds groan under most distress ?
Or why should pride humility make thrall,
And injuries the innocent oppress ?
Heavens ! hinder, stop this fate; or grant a time
When good may have, as well as bad, their prime !

Turning to the prose of this period, we recognise in it singularly little of first-class importance. Previous to Knox and Buchanan, there is only the anonymous *Complaynt of Scotland* (1549), still archaic in form, with little to commend beyond its isolated position and its virulent attack on England.

John Knox, of course, was a great personality in his way, but as a man of letters he is not considerable. A vigorous, truculent writer, his aim is religious and moral, and his *First Blast of the Trumpet against the Monstrous Regiment* (Government) *of Women* (1558) is more remarkable for its quaint title and uncompromising point of view than for any literary interest.

His contemporary, George Buchanan, has more claim upon the student of letters. For part of his life he lived in France, concerned in schoolmastering, among his pupils being Montaigne. Most of his work was written in Latin, and his English prose, at times suggesting an analogy with Ascham, though less clear and straightforward, is vigorous and polemical in trend.

James I has some claim as a writer of clear, forcible prose, with his *Counterblast to Tobacco*, and the *Basilicon Doron*; but the most distinguished name is that of Sir Thomas Urquhart, Knight of Cromarty (1611–60), a notable Royalist whose style has many of the interesting characteristics of Elizabethan prose, salted with national idiosyncrasies. He gave us a translation of Rabelais and some extraordinary works on scientific and literary subjects.

In approaching Allan Ramsay (1686–1758) we meet the pioneer in Scotland of that movement towards naturalism and passion in poetry that culminated in the Romantic Revival, finding in Burns its greatest exponent across the Border, and some half-dozen great names in English literature farther south.

Apprenticed to a wig-maker in Edinburgh, Ramsay

came across Watson's choice selection of Scottish lyrical verse, and this affected him much as the old ballad had affected Sir Philip Sidney.

Stirred up to write himself, he starts in a vein that is mostly satirical, and even when pathetic is more whimsical than sentimental. Dealing almost entirely with low life, he gives us a vigorous, realistic picture of Edinburgh types in the eighteenth century.

In addition to his lighter pieces, there is his pastoral drama *The Gentle Shepherd*, where he presents a picture of rustic life, somewhat conventionalised, it is true, to suit the requirements of the day, yet with a certain freshness and naturalness, and a pleasant humour that gives it distinction. He did a good deal of work in the matter of resettling old songs, but he was far happier in the lighter moods than in the sentimental. Yet his English lyrics enjoyed a fair popularity and, despite the commonplace character of much of his writing, his undoubted interest in Scots vernacular literature and his zeal in popularising it did a good deal to prepare the way for Burns.

A Song

My Peggy is a young thing,
Just entered in her teens,
Fair as the day, and sweet as May,
Fair as the day, and always gay.
My Peggy is a young thing,
And I'm not very auld,
Yet well I like to meet her at
The waulking of the fauld.

My Peggy speaks sae sweetly,
Whene'er we meet alane
I wish nae mair to lay my care,—
I wish nae mair of a' that's rare.
My Peggy speaks sae sweetly,
To a' the lave I'm cauld;
But she gars a' my spirit glow
At the waulking of the fauld.

Among other predecessors of Burns are William
Hamilton of Bangour, with his happily rhythmic
Braes of Yarrow ("Busk ye, busk ye, my bonny
bride"), 1724; George Halket, an Aberdeen schoolmaster and a Jacobite ballad-writer; the effective
song-writers Alexander Ross and John Skinner of
"Tullochgorum" fame. Of this gay effusion, indeed, Burns has said it was "the best Scots song Scotland ever saw". Another Jacobite singer is Alexander
Geddes, a man of considerable accomplishment, who
showed his scholarship in his translation of Theocritus
and Virgil and his humorous insight into rustic life in
his *Wee Wifukie*.

Many eighteenth-century Scottish songs familiar to
the modern reader are either anonymous or of doubtful authorship. *There is nae Luck aboot the Hoose*, for
instance, appeared about 1771. Its authorship is
uncertain, though James Beattie added two verses to
the original; but *I had a Hoose awa' there awa'*, *O'er
the Moor among the Heather*, are songs whose paternity
has never been determined. Lady Anne Barnard
(1750–1825) wrote *Auld Robin Gray*, while the ill-
fated figure of Robert Fergusson (1750–74) is perhaps

the most interesting personality, after Ramsay, in the period before Burns. His gift as a writer of vernacular verse was shown in his fifteenth year, while a student at St. Andrews; during his brief life he distinguished himself as a poet of urban life, especially the rough urban life and primitive jollities of Edinburgh towards the end of the eighteenth century.

These things are exhibited with humour and whimsical charm in *Auld Reekie, Wale of Ilka Town, Leith Races, Hallow Fair*.

His few experiments in rural subjects are equally happy, such as *To the Bee* and the sketch of a winter's night in a farm kitchen, entitled *The Farmer's Ingle*. At the age of twenty-four he died in a madhouse, but in his slender output he had already shown more imaginative promise and artistic excellence than any of his predecessors, though his work was necessarily less varied and extensive than Ramsay's.

Chapter Twelve

Philosophers from the Sixteenth to the Nineteenth Centuries

(i) Thomas Hobbes (1588–1679)

HOBBES entered Magdalen College, Oxford, in 1603, where he alleged geometry to be neglected in favour of the Black Art and where he " tooke great delight to goe to the bookbinders shops and lie gaping on maps ". Taking his degree, he became tutor to several distinguished families and was teacher of mathematics to Charles II. For twenty years he was in the household of the Earl of Cavendish, but published only a translation of Thucydides in 1628. His pupil dying in that year, he travelled abroad in a new tutorship. In Paris he saw, in a private library, " Euclid's Elements lay open and 'twas the 47th (proposition). He read the proposition. ' By God,' sayd he, ' this is impossible ' ". Finding his error, he fell in love with geometry and became convinced that all philosophical thought was capable of similar demonstration.

He returned to England in 1631, continued his studies while remaining tutor to various pupils, and circulated some of his theories in manuscript form.

In 1640 he went to France, apprehensive of the view the Long Parliament might take of his opinions. In 1651 he published *Leviathan*, not long after the appearance of two other philosophical works which were eventually published as one work in the eighteenth century (*Elements of Law, Natural and Politic*).

Hobbes determinedly taught that church government should be subordinate to the rule of the State. This view being even more inflammatory on the Continent than in England, he came home, was pensioned at the Restoration, and resided mostly with the Devonshire family.

In England he continued his studies in political and other branches of philosophy, publishing works on Society, on Man, and the *Questions Concerning Liberty, Law, and Chance* (1656), which involved him in great controversies. Eschewing Aristotelian method and striving to give philosophy a mathematical certitude by applying mathematical principles to his problems, he necessarily drew the fire of political thinkers, mathematicians, theologians, astronomers, and almost every writer of his day.

Ranking in importance with *Leviathan* was his *Behemoth : The History of the Civil Wars of England* (1679). Even this work did not satisfy his eagerness to write, for he followed it with a *Dialogue . . . of the Laws of England*. In 1681 he published verse translations of the *Iliad* and *Odyssey* of Homer. He later published a verse Church History and four years later his autobiography in Latin verse. Six years later, when he was ninety, he completed *Ten Dialogues of Natural Philosophy*. A year later he died.

In politics Hobbes opposed extreme absolutism to republicanism. In moral philosophy he held whatever is pleasant to be good, and only what is painful to be evil. He contended that man is essentially selfish and that gratification of self is the only motive by which man acts. It will easily be seen how a man whose system of thought led him to this conclusion inevitably held that there must be Leviathan, which is the absolute rule of one man or institution, to the support of which all men are bound as the only means of securing an ordered society.

Whatever the errors of his thought, he was the first to write an English classic of political science. He defined his terms and adhered to his definitions. His original views stimulated thought among his opponents.

As a writer he has considerable compression and an exact use of words. His imagination lightens his sometimes heavy and uneven sentences. Working always from one central idea, he writes with allusion, clarity, force.

As a thinker and as a writer, then, Hobbes had considerable influence. If his thought, for its inexactness, has not drawn many followers, it is yet true that, because of its lucidity, his style has been a useful model for his critics.

A contemporary of Hobbes, James Harrington (1611–77), opposed his theories in the eccentric, unexciting, but occasionally worthwhile *Oceana*. This is a description of a Utopia vastly different from Sir Thomas More's. Harrington held that an artificial equality of man should be imposed and that private possession should be limited. Opposed to extreme absolutism, he yet admitted the need for " one man " who should be a supreme ruler. Harrington's weakness as a writer is the inability of his prose to express the fullness of his imagination.

(ii) John Locke (1632–1704)

Born at Wrington, Somerset, and educated at Westminster and Christ Church, Locke chanced to meet Lord Ashley, Earl of Shaftesbury, and thereafter resided with this patron. In quietness he pursued the study of medicine and philosophy until Shaftesbury's downfall. Then, in 1683, he crossed to Holland. Returning on the accession of William III, he lived for some years with Sir Francis and Lady Masham, at Oates, in Essex, so that, like Hobbes, he was able to continue his philosophical speculations without disturbance or anxiety.

The great *Essay concerning Human Understanding* and the *Treatise of Government* appeared in 1690. Three years later he published *Thoughts on Education*. In 1704 he surmised that " the dissolution of the cottage was not far off ". It came on October 28. His practical and kindly nature was well illustrated by his will, which directed an inexpensive funeral so that the money saved might benefit the poor of the parish.

Locke's philosophical speculations had a simple origin. Realising that argument frequently led to no conclusion, he took a sheet of paper in order to write down those ideas with which the mind may conclusively grapple. The sheet grew to a volume which he was twenty years in writing. Briefly, his theory is that there are no innate ideas and that human thought may comprehend God (by a demonstrative knowledge), Man (by an intuitive knowledge), and Nature (by a " sensitive knowledge "). Furthermore, he believes that God enables the mind to have certainty as to some facts, but only probability about others. He reaches these conclusions from the premises that our ideas are formed either through sense perceptions (Ideas of Sensation), so that the basis of all knowledge is experience, or through reflection on these ideas (by which we form Ideas of Reflection). Consequently his theories leave a wide field of physical fact uncertain, since we can never ascertain the nature of any material fact, and he turns to Christian Revelation to supply the facts which the mind cannot discover unaided.

In order that man may be free to explore the spiritual world, he urged toleration of religious belief. From it he excluded Catholics (whom he regarded as the slaves of a foreign ruler) and atheists (whom he considered, by the nature of their beliefs, to repudiate the right to such exploration of the immaterial world).

Locke's political philosophy was similar to that of Hobbes in that he was an absolutist. He differed by stating that in return for his submission the individual must receive from the State or Ruler privileges as well as rights.   Thus he became an advocate of civil liberty in addition to freedom of conscience.

His main philosophical influence is due to the empirical element in his work—his insistence that experience is the basis of knowledge.   In this he was in keeping with the growth of scientific enquiry in his day.

As a writer he has the merit of lucidity.   Few writers of philosophical books have been so able to make their message intelligible to any reader.   Yet, when we have said this, nothing favourable remains. Every imaginative figure, every sign of wit or humour, every grace, Locke excluded from his prose, doubtless assured, by that intense feeling for what is practical which characterises him, that only the plainest and least-ornamented style is suitable to philosophical writing.   Such influence as he had on literary development must be admitted, then, to have contributed to the dullness of the writing which was done late in his time and after his death.   The Age of Dryden ended with a large sprinkling of earnest, gifted writers now buried in the dust of dullness, so that there is scarcely need to mention even the names of some of the best— Cudworth, Culverwel, Norris—men of merit in almost every way except as writers.

(iii) George Berkeley (1685–1753)

Born in Kilkenny, he became a Fellow of Trinity College, Dublin, and " revelled " in Greek and mathematics. He remained Fellow and tutor until 1713, by which time his most important books had been written. His *Essay towards a New Theory of Vision* appeared in 1709, followed by part of his *Treatise concerning Human Knowledge*. Three years later he visited London for the printing of *Three Dialogues between Hylas and Philonous*. The state of the country following the South Sea Bubble appalled him. Its misery he believed to be due to the decay of religious practice. In 1721 he issued an *Essay towards Preventing the Ruin of Great Britain*, and soon afterwards was appointed Dean of Derry. He at once devoted his ampler means towards the foundation of an educational colony in the Bermudas for the benefit of British colonists and American natives. Relying on a promise by Walpole that a grant would be made for the carrying out of his ideas, he voyaged to Rhode Island in 1729 to found a college. The promise was unfulfilled; the project collapsed. On his return, Berkeley entered the religious controveries of the time, but his next significant work was *The Theory of Vision*, in 1733, followed by an examination of Newton's mathematics in *The Analyst* (1734). Ten years later he published *Siris; a Chain of Philosophical Reflexions*. Here he freely expressed his views on numerous topics, especially on idealism, not omitting his favourite topic—the efficacy of tar-water as a panacea. He was made Bishop of Cloyne in 1734; he resided in his diocese until within a short time of his death, which occurred at Oxford in 1753.

Accepting Locke's view that the basis of knowledge is experience, Berkeley held that the perceptions of one sense are associated with those of another only by experience and that, consequently, our linking of them is arbitrary. As a result we can know only our thoughts; we cannot know anything other. At this crucial point, where Locke said that ideas represented things, Berkeley said that our ideas are the things. We do not know that there is anything beyond our ideas. In other words, we cannot say that anything material exists, but only that our ideas actually are the reality we think they represent. Incidentally, he said that God exists because He is the mind whose knowing gives reality to whatever else exists; we in turn are responsible for also knowing, and therefore giving existence to, the material world we think to be around us.

From the literary viewpoint, Berkeley is the finest of our philosophical writers. His prose has the charm and urbanity of Addison; his statements and arguments are distinguished by excellence of illustration and a fine irony; suavity of manner and clarity of statement are hall-marks of every page he wrote.

(iv) David Hume (1711–76)

The problem was taken over from Locke and Berkeley by David Hume, who built a system of philosophical scepticism on it. Described by his mother as " a fine, good-natured crater, but uncommon wake-minded ", Hume showed himself a man of genial generosity, acute perception, simplicity of taste, and scholarly inclinations. For many years he lived in Edinburgh with his sister, a maid, and a cat, finding books more necessary than a wife. His principal works are *Treatise on Human Nature* (1739), *Essays* (1742), *Human Understanding* (1748), *Principles of Morals* (1751), *Political Discourses* (1752), *History of England* (1754–61), *Natural History of Religion* (1757), *Essays and Treatises* (1770), *My Own Life* (1777), *Natural Religion* (1779).

Following Locke's empirical method of enquiry, Hume agreed with Berkeley that experience is the foundation of our knowledge. Beyond this point he differed by holding that the mind knows only two kinds of thoughts—the Impressions which are what our senses tell us, and the Ideas, which are the far weaker images, made by the mind, of the Impressions. Consequently we cannot infer any reality to exist merely because we have an idea of reality. He does not deny the possible existence of a material world but states that we cannot have certainty about it. In the same way he argues that we cannot know anything about ourselves, since the mind is not a self, but a rapidly changing bundle of perceptions necessarily in flux. He also denied Causality, observing that the sequence of *B* on *A* does not justify the conclusion that *A* necessarily causes *B*. In spite of this, he believed in a God, whose existence he held to be demonstrated by the design of the world.

His scepticism was far more destructive than the

apparently more revolutionary views of Berkeley, since he attacked the spiritual world—e.g. by denying the existence of an immaterial thing called mind, as well as the physical. In theological speculation he is vague, since he maintained (especially in the celebrated *Essay on Miracles*) that " mere reason " cannot prove the validity of Christianity. And outside mere reason he was not, he felt, obliged to seek any source of knowledge. In moral teaching we note with interest that he rejected the " self-interest " motive of Hobbes. Hume held—and it is characteristic of his nature that he did so—that we are motivated by what is useful or agreeable to ourselves or to others. The man who gave his salary as Keeper of the Advocates' Library, Edinburgh, to the blind poet Blacklock spends many pages in proving that there is merit in our being considerate of the welfare of our fellow men as well as in taking prudent care of our own. Part of the reward we enjoy for our conduct is " philosophic serenity ". One may reflect that Hume's contentment was perhaps more due to the generous gratification of his own good nature than to the philosophical approval his investigations later allowed him to concede.

As a thinker Hume has been most influential, especially among agnostic thinkers. As a writer, he is unexciting, but always polished, clear, ironical, and sometimes witty.

Among the lesser writers of the long period we have covered, merely factual accuracy justifies us in mentioning the Rev. Arthur Collier, whose book on the non-existence of an external world, in 1713, reached the same conclusion as Bishop Berkeley independently and by a different method; and the Rev. Conyers Middleton, whose book on the Patristic miracles denied their validity as firmly as Hume denied the validity of miracles in general. Hume declared that Conyer's work "eclipsed" his own essay on the subject.

A critic of Hume was Thomas Reid (1710–96), who built up a "common-sense" school of philosophy. He held that the objectivity of the external world is evident and immediately certain, since the validity of our sense perceptions and our reflections on them is unassailable. Hume read a manuscript of one of Reid's works, and returned it to him with the mild observation that "it is certainly very rare that a piece so deeply philosophical is wrote with so much spirit, and affords so much entertainment to the reader".

To include even one tenth of the writers on philosophy and theological speculation would, in this record of books of literary value, be a mistake. Interesting as many of them are, and overwhelmingly popular as some of them were, not even the ethical writings of Bishop Joseph Butler may be mentioned. In an age of free thought many minds searched for a faith; interesting as their investigations are, they are not necessarily literature. When so many new lines of thought were struck out, and when so many of them snarled up together, we must take our leave of controversialists, sceptical pessimists, deistical optimists, agnostic Catholics, and latitudinarian Protestants, and turn to William Law (1686–1761), who gave us a great classic of English mysticism.

Law was in all things an individualist. Charles Wesley was writing his 6,000 hymns, some of them worthy to be included in our national literature, and John Wesley was writing a diary not unworthy to be compared with that of Pepys. James Hervey was writing meditations in what has been called "the debased Jeremy Taylor style of literary architecture", and Augustus Toplady achieved the immortal hymn, "Rock of Ages".

Quietly puzzling out a way to lead a Christian life of faith, William Law took Orders and then, finding it impossible to accept the Oath of Allegiance to George I, he became a non-juror, thus forfeiting his living and his Cambridge fellowship. Rejected by the Church of England, in which he passionately believed, he became a powerful influence in the spiritual life of Methodism, although his theological views were fundamentally opposite to those of the Wesleys.

It is interesting to know that Law was tutor to the father of the historian, Edward Gibbon, and that he resided for many years with Gibbon's aunt, Hester, and another lady likewise given to quiet, prayerful living and good works. In such circumstances he published his *Practical Treatise on Christian Perfection* (1726) and his *A Serious Call to a Devout and Holy Life*,

Adapted to the State and Condition of All Orders of Christians (1728).

These books, especially the second, have been read by many generations of Englishmen and in them we may see the foundation of Evangelical thought. John Wesley was greatly influenced by them, until he discovered the author's attitude to the doctrine of Atonement. Then he turned rather to Henry More, whose *The Fool of Quality* he shortened and issued as *The History of Henry, Earl of Moreland*, a book more widely read than almost any other of Methodist interest.

Law turned from ascetical writing to mystical, coming strongly under the influence of Boehme. In *An Appeal to All that Doubt* (1740) and *The Way to Divine Knowledge* (1752) his mystical writing is seen at its best.

While the philosophers were arguing about the value of knowledge as it is in the senses and as it is in reflected ideas, Law took it that all knowledge was one, whether in the body or in the mind. Conflicts of experience and the perversities of human nature were, for him, only the meeting of those opposites by which alone progress is possible. It is not far-fetched to see in him a likeness to William Langland. Completely apart as both men were in their religious tradition and doctrine, both were at one in finding confusion in their times, difficulty in their personal lives, and certainty only in the thought that God must be served as the first duty of man. Both turned to

practice as the solution of their difficulties, in the
belief that good works and charity to all men are a
sound basis for a way of life, and that real unity and
beauty may be found only in holy living.

Law's literary expression is amazingly suited to his
purposes as a writer. Full of charm and felicity of
phrase, it is also fast moving, witty, and always persuasive. Through it shows a quiet certitude, a
kindliness towards men, a zeal as unassuming as it is
sincere, which adds qualities impossible to define.
They are qualities which have endeared his work to
philosophers and to the unlearned alike.

INDEX